MUSIC, MIND, AND EDUCATION

MUSIC, MIND, AND EDUCATION

KEITH SWANWICK

ROUTLEDGE
London and New York

First published in 1988 by
Routledge
a division of Routledge, Chapman and Hall
11 New Fetter Lane, London EC4P 4EE

Published in the USA by
Routledge
a division of Routledge, Chapman and Hall, Inc.
29 West 35th Street, New York NY 10001

British Library Cataloguing in Publication Data

Swanwick, Keith
    Music, mind, and education
    1. Schools. Curriculum subjects: Music
    I. Title
    780'.71

    ISBN 0-415-01478-6
    ISBN 0-415-01479-4 Pbk

Library of Congress Cataloging in Publication Data

Swanwick, Keith.
    Music, mind, and education

    Bibliography: p.
    Includes index.
    1. Music — Instruction and study. 2. Music —
Psychological aspects. 3. Music and society. I. Title.
MT1.S943 1988   780'.7   88-16102
ISBN 0-415-01478-6
ISBN 0-415-01479-4 (pbk.)

FOR
MAUREEN

Contents

Figures

Acknowledgements

I am grateful to London University Institute of Education for permission to draw on ideas published in my Special Professorial Lecture *The Arts in Education: Dreaming or Wide Awake?* (1983). Also to Cambridge University Press for access to material written jointly with June Tillman, 'The sequence of musical development: a study of children's composition', *British Journal of Music Education* 3 (3), November 1986.

Universal Edition (London) Ltd. have kindly given permission for the quotation from *The Rhinoceros in the Classroom* by Murray Schafer (1975). The text of the poem 'The parable of the old man and the young' is taken with permission from *The Collected Poems of Wilfred Owen*, published by Chatto & Windus (1967).

It has been possible to complete the work thanks to the Council of Institute of Education who generously allowed me a period of extended study leave in 1988.

Many of the themes running through this book have evolved over several years of lively contact with teacher colleagues, especially MA and research students at the university. I hope that they will find something of value here. In particular I must acknowledge Richard Frostick, who recently fanned the flames of my interest in Popper and also the work of June Tillman; without her research this book would be very different.

My secretary was Margaret Clements, who patiently and carefully helped me to work towards a final version of the text, skilfully negotiating the difficulties of incompatible word processors.

Introduction

Before embarking on the substance of this book, it seems permissible to make a brief sketch of how and why it came to be written.

At various times a musician, school teacher and a university professor, my particular good fortune has been in having opportunities to engage with music, people and ideas in lively ways, and to be constantly stimulated by the interaction of intellectual ideas and professional practice. Above all, I have enjoyed the illumination of artistic activity by philosophical, psychological and aesthetic enquiry. Even at the busiest and most engrossing times in school classrooms, or rehearsing and organizing groups of amateur and professional musicians, or embroiled in school and university politics, a necessary sense of being able to stand back, hold things in perspective and reflect upon the purpose of the 'business' has helped to preserve sanity and show a way forward.

I take it that this tendency is not unique and that everyone tries to understand the world, to make mental maps, to gather up the scattered elements of human experience. We all need to 'sort things out'.

It so happens that the job I now do in music education compels me to 'sort things out' in a fairly rigorous way. I cannot get away with looseness, vagueness or mere opinion in sessions with students or in conversation with colleagues. There is a feeling of being constantly driven on to explain, to interpret, to draw together ideas; in other words, to theorize. Not all of this pressure comes from people; some of it is exerted by ideas, theories or situations themselves. 'Come on', they say, 'sort us out.'

I think it possible to trace my personal major preoccupations, my 'sortings out', within music education as they have unfolded over three decades. During the 1960s, the intellectual magnet that drew my research interest towards it was, essentially, the problem of the nature of musical experience. The feeling that this was the central area needing to be opened up for music education was reinforced by an intuitive sense of the incredible power and mindmaking potential of music, an awareness amplified by resonances in the writings of Langer and others who managed to describe and almost, *almost* verged on explanations of what music really *is*. This intellectual quest was undertaken from a 'base camp' of teaching, rehearsing, performing and composing; activities against which the ideas always were tested.

1

This interest in a theory of music was challenged by the relatively new phenomenon of mass-distributed popular music, then beginning to be viewed with either alarm or curiosity by music educators. In *Popular Music and the Teacher* (1968), I did what I could to tease out the issues in a productive way, though not abandoning the idea of musical responsiveness to a sociological fate. It was, I believe, the first British attempt to take up the issue of pop music seriously in terms of music education.

By the early 1970s, British music education seemed riven by conflicting 'philosophies' — in effect various theories about music and the way people learn. These corresponded with a range of curriculum practice that made class music in schools appear almost arbitrary, though teaching in higher and further education hardly strayed from traditional assumptions and patterns of practice. 'Belief and action in music education' (1977) was an attempt to get these issues out into the open, while the main purpose behind *A Basis for Music Education* (1979) was to try to create a philosophical raft on which music education in schools and colleges might be floated. I was after a comprehensive theory which could be challenged, refined and put to work by music educators in a variety of practical settings. In *Discovering Music*, written with Dorothy Taylor (1982), these ideas were embodied in practical suggestions to show how they could help to generate principled curriculum activities.

For better or for worse, it is not hard to see the influence of some of these ideas, along with those of other colleagues, embodied in contemporary classroom activities, in the deliberations of advisers and inspectors, in the criteria of the British GCSE examination, in new 'A' Level proposals, in HMI documentation and in some of the recent developments in higher education. Working towards an understanding of the aesthetic and psychological basis of music and musical experience appears to have helped to facilitate a change of educational climate.

One thing seems plain: music educators now seem generally more able to deal with multiplying demands for accountability, more prepared to negotiate with the outside world, more articulate about their theories and practice: and so they need to be. Even more important, there seems to be increased awareness of the need to get to grips with the curriculum consequences of the aesthetic, artistic and affective significance of music.

At least I feel able to say that I have engaged with ideas as though they mattered, recognizing that they have a life, a vitality of their own. In this, I have been influenced by the wisdom of Karl Popper.

The expressionist believes that all he can do is to let his talent, his gifts, express themselves in his work. The result is good or bad, according to the mental or physiological state of the worker.

As against this I suggest that everything depends upon the give-and-take between ourselves and our work; upon the product which we contribute . . .

(Popper, 1972: 147)

In this book, this particular 'product', I want to sharpen up and develop earlier thinking, relating investigation into the nature of musical experience to the maturation, education and development of young people and to the undeniable fact that societies are, and always have been pluralistic, many-cultured. To adapt a famous biblical utterance: wherever two or three are gathered together, there we have a multi-cultural society! I intend this to be taken in two ways. Any group of people sustained by a common interest or a set of shared values — religious organizations; social clubs; occupational tribes of hunters, farmers or accountants — will develop customs, conventions and conversational manners of a more or less specialized kind, creating a sub-culture. At the same time, two or three people never share an absolute correspondence of ideology, social background or temperament; each individual is, so to say, electrically charged with his or her own biological and psychological current.

Just how individuals make their personal 'worlds' is really the sub-plot of this book, worked out for the arts and especially for music. Recognition of this process helps us to avoid stereotyping, the down-grading of individuality, the tendency to reduce personal 'style' to ethnic, national, or cultural cartoons. We also need to be alert to Popper's notion of 'products', remembering that musical products are themselves evidence of the need of each unique human individual to make and interpret the world through shared symbolic processes. This biological and psychological necessity transcends race, nationality and cultural bias. In this distinctively human enterprise, music — one of the great symbolic modes — plays its part.

No credible theory of music education can be sustained without an insightful analysis of music as an essential strand in the fibre of human experience. No sensitive practice of music education can take place without at least an intuitive grasp of the qualitative nature of musical response. No effective policy-making on curriculum content and evaluation or student assessment can be managed without a conscious awareness of what is central to musical experience. This applies as much to the curriculum in further and higher education as to schools.

One further presupposition is the acknowledgement that music exists outside of formal education in schools and colleges. It is therefore important to ask what the distinctive role of educational institutions might be, particularly that of schools, the main agents of compulsory education.

The thesis

After considering the necessity of coming to a cogent and workable theory for music education, I turn to a range of psychological work in search of keys which might unlock some of the secrets of music itself, trying to get closer to knowing what it is that makes music *musical*. This cannot be achieved by studying music as a kind of independent entity, as though musicological analysis could be separated from the psychology of musical perception and response. Music works through minds. The first task therefore is to identify the essential psychological elements that go to make up musical mind, that is to say, mind experiencing the world with music.

Although from this literature we can begin to get a glimpse into the nature of musical experience, the psychology of music has lacked a sense of direction and tended to wander about without a clear map, bereft of organizing principles. It has been waylaid by behaviourism and other psychological fashions and by attempts to measure musical abilities, very narrowly defined. Musical 'stimuli' have been reduced to fragments of sound bearing no relationship to music as we actually experience it.

It therefore becomes necessary to return to fundamentals, to reason out a positive view of the arts as part of the process of the development of mind and to expose the essential elements of musical apprehension and response, the heart of music-making and music-taking. Research into the musical behaviour of children at different ages confirms that these elements of musical mind emerge in a developmental sequence, a sequence dependent on opportunities, on the musical environment and on education. Music is not simply a pleasurable sensation giving rise to a physical 'knee-jerk' reaction, but involves cognitive processes and can be more or less understood by those responding to it.

The emergent theoretical template helps to organize thinking about music education in a more purposeful manner and it also allows us to map out, interpret and utilize psychological research into music in a more sharply focused way. Through this lens, it becomes possible to see ways through the complexities of generating and sustaining music education in a pluralist society, examining how curriculum activities are selected and framed by institutional constraints and teaching styles.

I shall argue that the major distinctive contribution to musical development made by formal institutions — schools and colleges — lies in the abstraction and practical exploration of clearly identified musical processes across a range of cultural 'for-instances', essentially in musical criticism. Because they are essentially symbolic entities, musical products can transcend both the individual self and the social community. Music is not simply a mirror reflecting cultural systems and networks of belief and tradition, but can be a window opening out to new possibilities.

With this declared model of musical mind and musical development, I approach the issue of accountability, considering how we might more sensitively assess the products of students and evaluate musical events within the context of schools and colleges.

1

In praise of theory — does it matter what we think?

> I am convinced that music is too powerful a subject to compromise its individuality to educational theory.
>
> (Peter Fletcher, *Education and Music* Preface, v)

It is sometimes tempting and often fashionable to take up an anti-intellectual stance and complain of theorizing, an activity which can be seen as remote from practicalities, in our case classrooms and living musical experience. Indeed, it is just as easy to find examples of dull and irrelevant theories, as it is possible to find instances of boring and trivial musical compositions or performances. There can also be tedious practical work, unilluminated by any sense of perspective and lacking any sense of purpose, sadly in need of a theoretical context. Doing things without thinking can be profitless, even hazardous.

I shall argue for the necessity, for the inevitability of theorizing, against the view quoted at the head of this chapter. Having said that music should not 'compromise its individuality to educational theory', Peter Fletcher goes on to develop what is, in reality, a detailed theory of music education. In a fairly prescriptive manner, he puts forward a theory based on what he calls 'musical intuition'. This is interesting and challenging, although we do not get to learn very much about the stuff of 'musical intuition'. I want to be more explicit than this and penetrate further into the nature of musical thought and behaviour. As it stands, I am not sure whether Fletcher really means musical intuition or just *his* personal intuition about music and music education.

The essential point here is that no human mind is free from the impulse towards theorizing, any more than human physiology can get by for long without breathing. If I am sent on a shopping expedition to buy vegetables and return with potatoes, carrots and cakes, I have either failed to understand the theoretical implications of the term 'vegetables', or I am deliberately going beyond instructions, perhaps determined to break some rule on diet. At another level, a teacher who believes that music education should be performance-orientated, or one who affirms that composing in small groups is the best way towards musical understanding, or another who emphasizes the importance of giving students individual instrumental instruction; all of these are implicitly working to theories about music and educational processes, whether or not they declare them publicly. Theories are not the opposite of practice but its basis.

A persuasive voice urging us to take theorizing seriously is that of the philosopher and scientist, Karl Popper, to whom I referred earlier. What he says seems as important for musicians and teachers as for scientists and philosophers, and, since I want to return later to the direct implications of his thinking for music education, it seems important here to at least hint at the essence of his work.

In an influential and powerful picture of the processes of human knowing, Popper conceives of three distinct 'worlds'. The first of these is the world of physical states, of objects and observable events, the world we experience as 'out there'; the second is the world of mental states, the world we tend to regard as subjective experience; the third world is the world 'of theories in themselves, and their logical relations; of arguments in themselves; and of problem situations in themselves' (Popper, 1972, 1979: 154). This last, 'World Three', is an autonomous world; it is a world of ideas, a world to which everyone contributes something but from which we all take much more. These ideas may take the form of scientific theories, philosophical reasonings, musical works, paintings, novels, poems, and so on.

All of the inhabitants of 'World Three' are the inevitable products of human thinking and imaginative speculation, inevitable in the same sense that spiders must make webs or birds must make nests. So you and I make theories, seeking explanations, looking for organizing principles by which to have, to hold and to interpret experience, trying to formulate concepts that may have predictive power. If we did not, we would hardly survive from day to day.

For Popper, a theory is not a system of unshakeable beliefs. Celebration and refutation of theories is the central activity of both the sciences and the humanities. It is, says Popper, 'from our boldest theories, including those which are erroneous, that we learn most'.

7

He gives as an example Beethoven 'theorizing' in the *Ninth Symphony*, problem-solving his way towards the novel *Finale*. In the same way, those of us who perform music can become aware that, for example, choice of a tempo can be seen as a form of theorizing. 'How might this passage work if the speed were to be fractionally slower or faster?' Setting a speed is surely the declaration of an organizing principle. The 'data', the musical gestures, have to be heard to 'fit', to make sense, to be expressively and structurally cohesive. If they aren't and if we are musically sensitive, then we abandon our tempo theory and try another.

Let us then resist theories that complain about theorizing as though it were an unnecessary waste of time. Secretaries of State for Education, Inspectors, Music Advisers, supervisors, and teachers all theorize, well or badly as the case may be, and like everyone else, they depend on 'World Three', on the thinking of others, though this may not always be acknowledged. Take the present preoccupation with testing and examinations as an example. The terms criterion referencing, and summative assessment, now so widely used in education, were not generated by politicians, or in Departments of Education at state or county level, but in universities and colleges.

In music education, the influential definitions of composition, performance, and audition (which some call 'listening') and the concepts of expressive character and structural elements did not materialize out of thin air but were given substance by the research of academics, the present writer for one. Although much work needs to be done to further realize the practical consequences of these ideas, indeed to understand them properly, it is undeniable that they have filtered into policy and curriculum practice, a process identified in music education by Marion Metcalfe (Abbs, 1987: 97–118).

Lively and critical theorizing is one defence we have against the arbitrary, the subjective, the dogmatic, and the doctrinaire; it is the way in which, as Popper says, we transcend ourselves.

> As it happens with our children, so it does with our theories:
> we may gain from them a greater amount of knowledge than
> we originally imparted to them.
>
> (Popper, 1972, 1979: 148)

This beautifully captures the sense of an autonomous realm of ideas. It is only when we begin to take seriously what our intellectual 'children' say, that we can begin to think and to talk productively with one another. Only then can any wisdom won by practical experience be formulated, shared and refined. Reflections on practice can only be exchanged through a mutually shared network of ideas, in the same way that conversations by telephone require an integrated system of wires, connections, amplifying and transmitting instruments. Anything else is non-communication and, although we may believe that we are holding professional conversations, we shall merely be uttering a miscellany of dogma. We can all recall 'discussions' of that kind! No profession can develop without debating key ideas or theories, bringing its assumptions out on to the table for public scrutiny. Music education is not exempt from this professional obligation.

Theories of music education

What kinds of theories of music education can we see at work around us? There is some evidence to suggest that, for good or ill, divergent practice and correspondingly diverse theories of music education are a feature of British music education.

From 1985 to 1987 I directed a research study, funded by the Gulbenkian Foundation at London University Institute of Education, where we looked carefully at the resource context and curriculum of 60 schools, 32 of them in some considerable detail (Institute of Education, University of London 1988). We found wide variation of classroom activity, sometimes influenced by the age of the pupils, or the type and location of the school. Quite commonly though, the curriculum seemed largely determined by the 'philosophy', that is to say, the theoretical perspective of individual teachers. For example, in one school, staff regarded themselves primarily as musicians rather than teachers and their view of the curriculum was indeed predicated on the standards and practices of the professional musical world of the western 'serious' tradition. In another school, staff saw their starting point as the pupils' motivation towards pop music. For a third school, the major activity was composing in small groups. As it happens, these were all secondary schools.

When we looked at what was *excluded* from curriculum practice, we found one school where pupils were 'never' asked to actually *play* any music and two schools in which it was estimated by the teachers that pupils 'rarely' sang. Fifteen of the sixty teachers said that they did not expect children ever to sing at sight. Sixteen did not ask pupils to compose, either with or without notation. Ten teachers 'rarely' had children listen to recorded music and six reported that they had no regular access to equipment on which to play recordings.

Observation of over 100 hours of teaching confirmed this impression of wide divergence: there were schools in which the most common working situation was composing in pairs and small groups, while in others — mainly primary schools — the teachers tended to organize performance or skill practice in whole classes. At least one teacher in each case categorized him- or herself as one who would 'never' use classical music or jazz, pop, rock or folk, contemporary or 'ethnic' music. As to singing, of the 147 lessons we observed, more than half included no singing at all.

There was then considerable divergence over musical idioms, classroom organization and the proportion of time spent on different activities, although there appeared to be on the surface a fairly broad consensus view of the curriculum. The existence of such a range of practice seemed to depend at least in part on what 'philosophy' of music education was held by particular teachers and some gave us an explicit rationale for their curriculum decisions.

It is worth sketching in some music curriculum 'philosophies', partly because they to some extent represent these divergent patterns of belief and professional practice that can be found in British schools, and, to some extent, in further and higher education. They are essentially theoretical schemes that arise out of and feed back into educational practice. A more positive reason for this brief examination is that they represent the three central pillars of music education: a concern for musical traditions; sensitivity to students; awareness of social context and community. I want to stress that these are not descriptions of individual teachers at work or even necessarily the ideas of particular writers. They are strands of thought and practice gathered into conceptual bundles to make theoretical harvesting a little easier.

Traditional values

Perhaps the oldest and best established theory of music education is that which emphasizes that pupils are inheritors of a set of cultural values and practices, needing to master relevant skills and information in order to take part in musical affairs. Schools and colleges can be seen to be important agents in this process of transmission. According to this theory, the task of the music educator is primarily to initiate students into recognizable musical traditions. This is a position that was until recently well-established and generally accepted.

Clear signs of the presence of this theory may include commitment to the value of learning to play a musical instrument, to musical literacy and familiarity with a repertoire of 'masterworks', or the work of master-musicians. A fine example is the work of Kodály and the extensive materials that form his *Choral Method*. This highly structured, sequential approach was intended primarily to develop musicianship through singing, especially sight-singing. He was convinced that every child should learn to read music and articulate it vocally, otherwise: 'Millions are condemned to musical illiteracy, falling prey to the poorest of music' (Kodály, 1974: 119–204). For Kodály, pupils are to be initiated only into music of 'unquestioned quality', beginning with (in his case) the folk traditions of Hungary and proceeding eventually to encounter the best music of the European classical tradition.

In the less rigorous atmosphere of many British schools, some teachers still feel that children should at least come into contact with 'good' music, should have some idea of how staff notation functions, should acquire some ability to aurally and visually recognize standard instruments and ensembles and should know something about important musicians and their work. Whenever possible, children will be encouraged to take up a musical instrument, thus gaining direct access to a valued tradition. Those secondary teachers and college lecturers who see things in this way may tend to regard themselves as musicians first and teachers second. One of the strongest recent advocates of this theory is Peter Fletcher, and he extends the range of traditions to what he calls 'ethnic' music, a policy that is culturally and musically necessary, although difficult to organize and to resource (Fletcher, 1987).

A frequent accompanying characteristic of the traditional theory is a belief in the value of competition and assessment. Of all the arts, music is the most often and rigorously examined. Not only does music find a place among the usual school and college examinations but there are also large independent examining systems throughout the English-speaking world, from Britain to Australia. In 1976 there were over 244,000 examination entrants for the Associated Board alone, more than double the entry of ten years before. In 1986 the figure was in excess of 262,000. The great majority of entrants were pianists, a high proportion were violinists, and clarinettists. All this practical activity, along with the 'theory' examination — which is not theory at all but is mainly concerned with the rules of musical notation — bears witness to the strength of the traditional view of music education; a belief enshrined in a highly articulated and influential assessment system.

A natural extension of this policy is the provision of special opportunities for those who show promise, through music centres, music schools, junior tuition at music colleges and a chance to excel at festivals and competitions.

Such a theoretical network is very powerful and exceedingly attractive. Its values are shared by a number of parents and politicians. Teachers who have been musically trained, for example, as a violinist within western traditions or as a sitar player in a tradition of the Indian sub-continent, are particularly well equipped and confident to pass on their knowledge and skills within these traditional boundaries. Teaching objectives are reasonably clear and criteria for assessment are to hand. It is not so hard to tell, for instance, whether a student makes progress on the trombone or the tabla: identifiable musical skills must be demonstrated.

Above all, there is a set of generally accepted educational aims and procedures. For example, in violin teaching, a long line stretches back from Suzuki and Rolland, through Doflein and others, to Mozart's father and beyond. Minor disagreements there may be as to the *how* and the *what*; the particular method of instruction and the material that might best be used; but rarely over the purpose, the *why*.

A problem with the practical effect of this theory is that it sometimes sits uncomfortably in compulsory education in school classrooms, where there is great cultural diversity. A not unknown result is a diet of popular classics on disc, of mainly unison singing — rarely the rigour of sight-singing, and of some information about music and musicians. Where this is not coupled in the mind of any student with the impact of actual music-making and music-taking relating to experience outside of school, the effect can be of a curriculum which resembles the scraps under a rich man's table, the cold left-overs of other people's meals, often unappetizing. Meanwhile, the musician/teacher's mind is elsewhere, perhaps planning the next rehearsal or performance with the elective groups, where most of the real work is thought to be done — outside of the classroom timetable and possibly outside of school altogether.

A further cautionary note has to be sounded. Students who are given opportunities to learn to play an instrument, through LEA schemes or private tuition, sometimes appear to become bogged down in a morass of notation or manipulative difficulties and either give up altogether or carry on playing in a mechanical and uncommitted way. The Swiss educator, Jaques-Dalcroze, found conservatoire music students lacking in fluency and expressiveness. They struggled to play technically correctly, but lacked a feeling of rhythmic involvement and musical sensitivity. His ambition was to have students feel music through physical movement, to play musically. Later on I shall return to what it is to play music musically, but for the moment want only to register the point that playing an instrument is not inevitably the way into meaningful musical engagement, unless teachers are very sensitive. Take, for instance, the experience of Bernard Levin who, put to violin lessons as a boy, found the experience decidedly unrewarding, complaining that too many children 'fall into the hands of teachers' who have no idea of what music really *is*. 'For two and a half years I laboured at this joyless thing called music without so much as learning the name of a single composer, or indeed discovering that such people existed' (Levin, 1981: 4).

Yet, a tremendous amount of good work has been accomplished by the light of this theoretical lamp. Young people have learned to play and sing and frequently have developed an understanding and love for music as a consequence. As a result, musical activity in Britain is acknowledged across the world, even if it is largely as a consequence of activities taking place outside of timetables and the school curriculum.

Focus on children

Over the past forty years or so, an alternative perspective on music education has gained ground, a theory which emphasizes the qualities of 'expression', 'feeling' and 'involvement'; shifting our attention from the student as 'inheritor' to the student as 'enjoyer', 'explorer', 'discoverer'. This 'child-centred' perspective owes much to Rousseau and to the pioneers of education for younger children, especially Pestalozzi and Froebel and to the American philosopher, John Dewey.

Music's first internationally recognized 'progressive' educator was the composer, Carl Orff. His emphasis (in the 1950s) was that musical involvement should be immediate and for everyone. Notational skills and instrumental instruction were subordinated to improvisation and the development of musical imagination.

Performing skills were to be acquired almost ritualistically in groups, with imitation and invention as positive and negative poles at the core of his 'method'. Orff was convinced that children could be encouraged to be creative by returning to fundamentals, to what he called 'elementals'. They should handle basic musical ideas, especially melodic and rhythmic patterns: the music that they make should be 'near the earth', natural and very physical. Music should also become reunited with movement, dance and speech (Orff, 1964 and Keetman, 1974).

Throughout the 1960s, this theoretical perspective was further developed and refined, stressing the creativity of children rather than received traditions. In Britain during the late 1960s and early 1970s, an influential advocate was John Paynter. In Canada, another composer, Murray Schafer, developed a similar position; while in the USA, detailed implications for the school music curriculum were articulated by Ronald Thomas in the *Manhattanville Music Curriculum Program* (1970).

This fundamental theoretical shift requires us to see children as musical inventors, improvisers, composers; either in order to encourage something called 'self-expression', or, more credibly, as a direct way of coming to understand how music actually works through activities calling for decision-making, handling sound as an expressive medium. One consequence of this theory is that the teacher's role is transformed from that of musical 'director' to that of pupil facilitator: stimulating, questioning, advising and helping, rather than showing or telling.

Helpful as this perspective is, it was thought by some to bring with it the risk of aimlessness, a *cul de sac* of experimentation without development. The success of such an approach relies on teachers being exceedingly sensitive to the musical products of the students. And indeed, it is these musical products that we must always keep centre-stage. As Popper reminds us, it is only *products*, things we say or make, that enable us to communicate with one another. We cannot see internal psychological processes at work unless there is some outward manifestation, some visible, audible, or tangible object; a perceptible event. We are not able to respond to the musical processes of students unless they play something or, possibly, even say something to us.

We have to be wary then of theorizing loosely about products and process, perhaps assuming that a product is necessarily always finished, rehearsed, notated, carved into stone. Not so. Our products are always in a sense provisional, open to criticism, to

change, to development and to reinterpretation. They are simply
the form taken by ideas: processes having shape and substance.
Once we recognize this, then we can also acknowledge that the
products of other people are important too: to borrow a telling
phrase from E.M. Forster, they feed our minds. A music curriculum
based on children experiencing *only* their own musical products
would starve and impoverish musical insight and development. Imagine what happens to children's acquisition of language if they
only talk with their own age-group.

The great virtue about the 'child-centred' theory of music education, stressing as it does the individuality and creativity of each child,
is that we are encouraged to look and listen more carefully to what
students actually *do*.

Respecting alternative traditions

The extension of schooling into young adulthood, the fragmentation of traditional rural communities and the increasing uprooting
and migration of people from across the world to new homes; these
and other factors make it impossible to specify what the common
cultural tradition of school and college communities may be.
Although this is not a new phenomenon, the processes of cultural
change and the transplantation of cultural practices has been
accelerated by mass transportation and rapidly evolving communication systems. We are all, in a sense, 'cultural refugees' and
may find it difficult to identify our roots.

A third and more recent theory of music education lays stress
on helping students to find and lay down cultural roots within the
new traditions of Afro-American musics that have permeated the
world since jazz and onwards. If there is such a thing as a common
culture of our own time, it is that which is sustained and, literally
as well as metaphorically, broadcast through the media of radio and
television, amplified by audio and video tape. The mass media do
come some way towards making communal, shared experiences,
an electronic folk-culture, orally transmitted and aurally received,
woven into the fabric of our everyday lives. A teacher would surely
be mistaken to ignore these widely shared traditions, where syncopations mingle with melismatic vocalizing, with synthesized sound
production and transformation and with a harmonic repertoire
substantially derived from the European classical tradition. It is also
salutary to observe just how much music children actually *learn*

15

through these experiences without necessarily having formal teaching.

This position was developed by Graham Vulliamy (Vulliamy and Lee, 1976), among others, and earlier in *Popular Music and the Teacher* (Swanwick, 1968). Teachers, said Vulliamy, had ignored the tremendous musical possibilities of the Afro-American traditions and tended to look down on music other than that of the 'classical' heritage, access to which was usually through skill with staff notation. Opportunities must therefore be created for students to develop instrumental and improvisational skills and to acquire stylistic sensitivity to jazz, to rock and to pop music and — a natural extension of the position — to the music of Asia and other regions. Music education thus begins to have relevance for pupils in the twentieth century.

A major issue here is that we are not thinking about one alternative musical culture but about a pluralism. Music is frequently involved in the process of marking out cultural territories. Different musics have their own audiences, their own radio channels and their own classificatory sections in record shops. What is the music teacher to do when students come to school committed to reggae, to soul, to Indi-pop, to ska or punk rock? The traditional theory in its oldest form has an answer: ignore such music and carry on striving for high standards in worthwhile music, hoping that students will eventually come to see the value of it all. One version of the child-centred theory also has an answer: in general music classes at least begin by having children explore sound and its expressive possibilities, rather than by initiating them into the skills and stylistic practices of specific musical idioms.

One major difficulty for the practical consequences of this culturally broad-based theory lies in the sheer diversity of musical styles, each with its own set of technical and stylistically accepted procedures. Which styles should and can be made available in education? How is a solitary music teacher in school to cope with the range? By what principles of critical selection are particular musical activities reckoned to be worthy of a place in the curriculum, given the limitations of time? How is such a curriculum to be resourced?

It does matter what we think

This brief sketch of three influential theories of music education has a purpose behind it. It may be only a rough and ready map of the theory and practice of music education in Britain but the crucial values of respecting musical traditions, individual creativity and social relevance present a challenge to any attempt to evolve a set of serviceable ideas for the future.

Of course, many teachers operate a 'pick and mix' curriculum, trying to select from the range of options those things that appear to 'work'. The general picture is of a music curriculum in schools that is somewhat arbitrary, depending on one of several theoretical belief systems or on the immediacy of what resources and know-how are available. As a basis for any kind of curriculum or for educational planning, such a medley of themes hardly approximates to an orchestrated policy. In our 1985–7 research project, the invitation to 60 teachers to name up to five items of class material in current use produced over 130 titles, 25 of these in service across both primary and secondary schools. Even so, many teachers said that they needed to generate their own material. This diversity, combined with the differing curriculum content and teaching style, might be said to represent rich seams of imaginative teaching. On the other hand, it could be in part due to uncertainty arising from lack of a policy on curriculum development and an adequate theory of music education.

Notice how hard such words as policy and theory are to the British ear. We tend to fall about in an attitude of distrust at the mere mention of such ungracious ideas; they seem to run against our inclination to let things alone and our trust in the inventiveness of teachers and the luck of the draw as far as resources are concerned. The result of this is that, when there is enthusiasm and good fortune, music education goes with a 'swing'. And when there isn't . . .? Of course, ultimately all depends on the teacher to find the magic spell that releases the energies of music and of students. But we ought not to rely totally on charismatic wizardry: we need to plan a little more for consistency of effectiveness; we ought to have sensitively formulated curricula with a clear rationale; it does matter that we think together about music education.

My purpose in the following chapters is to try to formulate ideas that relate strongly to the nature of music itself, to human psychology and to social settings. Naturally, I do not start with a blank sheet of paper. As we have seen, there are already theories waiting for attention and each has its 'history' and value system. The task is to try to bring together those ideas which seem most powerful and fertile, to reshape them, and offer them back to 'World Three'.

The crucial questions will be: Why are the arts important

human activities? What is musical intuition, or musical knowing? How does this develop in childhood and beyond? How best can we plan and operate a purposeful music curriculum in a pluralist society?

2

What makes music musical?

The shaking air rattled Lord Edward's membrana tympani; the interlocked malleus, incus and stirrup bones were set in motion so as to agitate the membrane of the oval window and raise an infinitesimal story in the fluid of the labyrinth. The hairy endings of the auditory nerve shuddered like weeds in a rough sea; a vast number of obscure miracles were performed in the brain, and Lord Edward ecstatically whispered 'Bach!' He smiled with pleasure, his eyes lit up.

(Aldous Huxley, *Point Counterpoint*: 38)

Sound and music

What are these 'obscure miracles' that transform Lord Edward from a set of vibrating tissues to a person responding positively to Bach? Having some insight into these processes of musical perception and response is a professional necessity for teachers, who need to know something of how people respond to music, and also for musicians, if they are to be sensitive to their art and to their audience.

In order to gain access to these miracles, I need to refer to work in the psychology of music, though it is not my intention to systematically review this literature, a service which has already been performed by others, notably Davies (1978), Shuter-Dyson and Gabriel (1981), Deutsch (1982), Sloboda (1985) and Hargreaves (1986). Instead, I shall draw attention to what seem to be significant features of this work and try to identify those findings and theories that make sense, both from musical and educational perspectives.

The psychology of music has seen several shifts of emphasis

19

over the last fifty years. One reason for this has been the lack of a robust conceptual framework; experiments and observations have been conducted without any overview or sense of priority. Workers in the field have sometimes appeared to forget that the central problem is to explain 'the structure and content of musical experience' (Sloboda, 1986). An exception to this is Carl Seashore, whose classic book, *The Psychology of Music*, is both wide-ranging and well-principled (Seashore, 1938). Generally though, psychological work in music and music education has appeared to neglect the central problem and has been without a shared and unifying theory. From the perspective of the special area of child-development, Hargreaves complains that there are virtually 'no coherent psychological theories of the specific developmental processes underlying children's musical perception, cognition or performance' (Hargreaves, 1986: 3).

Early investigations tended towards a very simplistic, almost mechanistic view of human engagement with music. The most obvious way to investigate the effects of music seemed to some to be to try to find a correspondence between sound and its direct effect on the human physiology. The shortcomings of this methodology are as obvious to us as they were to Aldous Huxley as he describes what is happening to Lord Edward.

There are great over-simplifications propping up the assumption that there is an observable physical change for every sound event, let alone that we might measure such changes. In spite of these difficulties, a number of investigators have used standard medical equipment in an attempt to measure and record the direct effects of music on human physiology. Earlier experiments are optimistically described by Ida Hyde.

> It has been discovered that cardio-vascular functions are reflexly stimulated concomitantly with psychological effects of music and that, through the use of the Einthoven string galvanometer, and sensitive sphygmomanometers, the physiological reactions that have been excited by different sorts of music can be measured and compared.
>
> (Hyde, in Schoen, 1927)

This kind of approach has all the paraphernalia of scientific method, with dials and meters giving out readings of changes in blood-pressure, pulse, respiration, galvanic skin response, and so on. Unfortunately, matters are not quite so straightforward and certain complications which became apparent to Hyde are still with us. A great deal depends on the state of health of the auditor, on the environment, on the degree of alertness or fatigue of the subject, on the degree to which the music used is familiar, and on the previous musical experience of the subjects. Generally speaking, music does tend to increase rates of pulse and respiration, though not always (Lundin, 1953: 134). However, the responses of musicians are likely to be less predictable than those of subjects picked up 'off the street', which is something of a nuisance to investigators (Hunter, 1970).

Even the gross physiological effects described by Sargant have to be viewed with caution and not taken as typical of musical response.

It should be more widely known that electrical recordings of the human brain show that it is particularly sensitive to rhythmic stimulation by percussion and bright light among other things and certain rates of rhythm can build up recordable abnormalities of brain function and explosive states of tension sufficient even to produce convulsive fits in predisposed subjects. Some people can be persuaded to dance in time with such rhythms until they collapse in exhaustion.

(Sargant, 1957: 92)

Certainly, the nervous system can be overstimulated by *sound*, something many of us know from experiences in discos. But most music does not reach these levels of direct physiological agitation and other ways have to be found of probing its psychological effects and the ways in which it is perceived.

This preoccupation with the physical properties of sound has had an effect on the formulation of musical curricula, especially in North America. It is still possible to find teaching programmes based on psychological correlates of the sound wave, as though it were possible to design a curriculum by building up musical understanding from little bits of acoustic material. The following table shows the relationship; the terms in the right-hand column still linger on in music teaching programmes. There seems to be a deep-seated wish to generate a curriculum structure from the materials of pitch, loudness, rhythm and timbre.

PHYSICAL   PSYCHOLOGICAL
a) frequency   pitch
b) intensity   loudness
c) form   timbre
d) duration   time

The main difficulty about attempting to map out music education in terms of the psycho-acoustical phenomena of pitch, timbre and so on, is similar to that inherent in investigations relying on physiological measures. Both tend to deal with musical *materials* stripped of the *elements* of character and structure. (On this distinction see Swanwick, 1979.)

Other early studies, while not relying on physiological measures, also show this concentration on musically unstructured and fairly characterless sound material. Myers and Valentine carried out experiments with single tones and bichords, work modelled to some extent on that of Bullough who investigated single colours (Myers and Valentine, 1914: Bullough, 1906). Valentine tried to find out if subjects would agree on descriptions of the emotional effect of single intervals (Valentine, 1962). They did not, something which is unsurprising, since isolated sound material of this kind tends to be what each individual chooses to make of it. For example, the minor third in one of those experiments was described as 'sad' or 'plaintive' by eleven people, as against twenty-six who thought that the major third had that character. Musical materials are notoriously ambiguous. Within western tonality, a minor third can be heard as the upper half of an incomplete major triad and a major third as part of a minor chord. Even at this impoverished level of musical experience, music listeners bring with them their own set of expectations.

From the 1940s onwards, the field of the psychology of music is littered with 'ability' tests and their evaluation. Some researchers attempt to include an 'appreciation' component, for example, Wing (1948); but many stay on the safer ground of testing the ability to identify pitch changes or count the number of notes in chords or discriminate between different timbres, sometimes asking for the comparison of melodic or rhythmic fragments on the basis of 'same' or 'different' (Lundin, 1949; Bentley, 1966).

A literature search, carried out in 1981 for the APU/DES Aesthetic Development Exploratory Group, confirms that tests in music tend to focus on aural discriminations or contextual factual knowledge (unpublished review, 1981). Very little work was identified which attempted to assess what the Group called 'Artistic Appraisals' — perception of expressive character and structure.

These limited forms of investigation into musical response somehow miss the whole point of what music really can mean to people: all of the richness is lost. Just as increase in pulse rate or respiration by themselves tell us little about the perceptual and affective worlds of the subjects; so correct or incorrect identification of pitch change or the number of notes in a chord only begins to scratch the surface of how people construe and respond to music. The listening agenda is just not the same.

Some of the earlier psychologists did attempt to recognize a range of different ways of taking music, even if it led to fairly crude categorizations. Ortmann divided up the responses of listeners into 'types' (Schoen, 1927), while Valentine (1962) came to divide what he called an 'associational' way of listening to music into two subsets: 'fused' (related with the music), and 'non-fused' (a freer play of fantasy). In other areas too, there was a similar move: for example the influential visual art educator, Herbert Read, was concerned to equate four categories of children's paintings and drawings with the four function-types of Jung: thinking; feeling; sensation; intuition (Read, 1956). From a musical angle and quite comprehensively, Philip Vernon listed seven categories of musical response (Vernon, 1933):

1. Physical (the actual sensation of the sound)
2. Free trains of thought (day-dreaming to music)
3. Emotional reaction (especially dramatic or visual associations)
4. Muscular reaction (including the delicate and complex adjustments that attend every perception)
5. Synaesthesia (particularly the link of musical key and visual colour)
6. Auditory images and intellectual processes (analytical and technical)
7. Social and temperamental factors

Such a categorization of the ways in which we respond to music is helpful to the extent that it moves away from 'types'. Most people will certainly make a mixed response and we ought to avoid labelling them. The trouble with all of this early psychological work is that it needs to be taken up into a cohesive scheme; it wobbles about without a theoretical foundation, often without any idea, as Levin says, of what music really *is*, something I want to try to remedy throughout the rest of this book.

Even so, we can begin to see that this brief sketch of some of the early concerns of the psychology of music, helps to begin to map out features of the landscape of musical experience. Sound itself does indeed impress itself upon us, especially above certain levels of loudness. Beyond this, we may take up an associative attitude, connecting what we hear perhaps with a colour, an event or, possibly, another sound — such as a police siren. Alternatively, we may frame musical experience within an externally imposed classification system; such as we find in ability tests, or when we are asked such things as 'is this piece in triple time? in a major key? played on what instruments? from what culture?'

These levels of response, while they may be thought to serve certain psychological or educational purposes, may detain educators, as they have constrained many psychologists, from moving forward to consider interesting sounds as expressive gestures embodied in coherent forms; which is what music essentially *is*. We must avoid a reductionist attitude, imagining that we build up musical experience from rudimentary atoms: that, for example, we first perceive intervals or single tones and that musical lines or textures are assembled in our minds only after analysis of the component parts has taken place. The converse is surely true. Analytic description is a different perceptual and conceptual mode which may have some value, but may also divert us from phrase, from expressive gesture, from the play of musical structure, from the coherence and sweep of musical passages. It is to these elements that we now turn.

Responding to expression

Presumably the notes which we hear at such moments tend to spread out before our eyes, over surfaces greater or smaller according to their pitch and volume; to trace arabesque designs, to give us the sensation of breadth and tenuity, stability or caprice.

(Proust, 1913: 288)

Studies of the expressiveness of music inevitably run into one major obstacle: any account by people as to how expressive character is perceived will inevitably be *metaphorical*, poetical rather than analytic. This quotation from Proust is an illuminating instance of this.

Here again, there is a history of psychological investigation. One of the earlier attempts was made by Esther Gatewood (in Schoen, 1927). She compiled a list of possible effects music might have on listeners, such as sad, serious, amused, rested, longing, patriotic and irritated. People were given a questionnaire on which those words were to be checked off in response to short, fairly popular pieces. A comment by Langer in *Philosophy in a New Key* pinpoints a doubtful assumption behind such work.

The results of such experiments add very little to the well-known fact that most people connect feelings with music, and (unless they have thought about the precise nature of that connection) believe that they *have* the feelings while they are under the influence of the music, especially if you ask them which of several feelings the music is giving them.

(Langer, 1942, 1957: 181–2)

Not only then is the language of musical description essentially metaphorical, but there is a distinction to be made between how a person believes music makes him or her *feel* and how the character of the music *itself* is perceived. For example, it would be perfectly possible for a piece of music to be perceived to have about it a general air of 'cheerfulness', but on that account be 'irritating' to a particular listener who may be feeling cynically disposed at the time; or for music to be heard as 'solemn' or 'patriotic' and to make an outsider feel 'amused' by its pretentiousness.

It has been argued that words are able to represent things for us because 'they produce in us some replica of the actual behaviour' (Osgood et al., 1957). In music, how is any such 'replica' mediated to us? Langer distinguishes between 'an emotion directly felt and one that is contemplated and imaginatively grasped'; but how is an 'emotion' presented in music and how is it identified and contemplated (Langer, 1957, 1970)? What remnant of remembered experience is activated or retrieved when we respond to the 'content' of music?

An imaginative answer is to be found in the work of Vernon Lee (Vernon Lee, 1932). In a series of case studies, she investigated ideas people have about music. She divided the responses of her subjects into two main categories, 'listeners' and 'hearers'. 'Listening', she tells us, takes place when one is 'taking stock of something which is moving and changing and in so far as it is accompanied in him who listens by a sense of high and complex activity'. 'Hearers', on the other hand, tend to day-dream and allow attention to wander away from the music. She makes it quite clear that the division into types is not really a matter of how people listen, but of their *attitude* towards the activity. 'Listeners' know that they are inattentive from time to time and tend to regard this as a failing: 'hearers' 'rarely admit that they have lapses of attention' and in any case tend not to think of music as requiring sustained concentration.

Vernon Lee found the most positive and illuminating views among her 'listeners', who spoke of music 'chasing away fatigue', bringing the 'keenest inner excitement or exaltation', a 'strong element of pleasure', a 'special profound emotion'. From this evidence, she is able to offer an operational model to account for those 'replicas' of life situations, drawing particularly upon the work of Henry Head and his concept of '*postural schemata*'. To quote Head directly:

> Every recognizable [postural] change enters into consciousness already charged with its relation to something that has gone before, just as on a taximeter the distance is presented to us already transformed into shillings and pence. So the final product of the tests of the appreciation of posture, or of passive movement, rises into consciousness as a measured postural change.
>
> For this combined standard, against which all subsequent changes of posture are measured before they enter consciousness, we propose the word 'schema'. By means of perpetual alterations in position we are always building up a postural model of ourselves which constantly changes.
>
> (Head, 1920: 605–6)

This may sound very abstract, but the reality of what Head is describing is easily illustrated. For instance, we know that people unfortunate enough to lose a leg by accident or surgery for some time afterwards complain of pain in the missing limb — an unkind irony. From this we know that such a person has a 'postural model' which still includes a *schema*, a representation, a replica of the leg in the central nervous system. Millions of previous sensations and actions have left behind persistent images.

26

Vernon Lee suggests that music could be analogous to these *schema* (literally the 'ghosts') of past movements. In music we can discern an immense range of manner of movement: reaching out, retraction, coalescence, extrusion, integration, disintegration, the rhythms of development and growth which are fundamental to all living forms. The schemata of a reaction, a stance, a muscular set, an emotion or a gesture could conceivably be presented in what Hanslick called the 'sounding forms' of music and we might, to some extent, empathize with them. We do not need to confine ourselves to thinking about particularly strong feelings or emotional states. Every perception involves an element of physical, muscular adjustment, a modification of kinaesthetic position, and any physical or 'mental' activity will leave a residual postural trace, including the activity we call thinking.

The distinction between 'hearer' and 'listener' has a bearing on this. To give an example, let us assume that someone attends closely enough to music to recognize at a certain point a particular 'attitude' or 'gesture'. By definition, the 'hearer' is likely to wander off into memories of situations in his or her own life or perhaps contemplate some biographical detail of the composer or performer, or admire the hat of someone in front. These activities will be regarded as distractions by a 'listener'. Thus, Bernard Shaw found his mind wandering towards remembered Irish funerals whenever he heard the *Eroica* symphony funeral march.

> Now the sorest bereavement does not cause men to forget
> wholly that time is money. Hence, though we used to pro-
> ceed slowly and sadly enough through the streets or terraces
> at the early stages of our progress, when we got into the open
> a change came over the spirit in which the coachmen drove.
> Encouraging words were addressed to the horses; whips were
> flicked; a jerk all along the line warned us to slip our arms
> through the broad elbow straps of the mourning-coaches . . .
>   It is that fatal episode where the oboe carries the march
> into the major key and the whole composition brightens and
> steps out, so to speak, that ruins me. The moment it begins,
> I instinctively look for an elbow strap . . .
>   (Laurence, 1981, Vol. 3: 134)

Shaw — very much a 'listener' — tells us that he would then wake up and realize regretfully that he had, for several pages of the score, not attended to a note of the performance.

One of the reasons why music may appear to 'mean' various things to different people lies in the degree to which specific experiences are associated with music. If we are day-dreaming, then a musical gesture will set off a string of personal idiosyncratic associations. If we take up the attitude of a 'listener', then, whilst recognizing the character of a particular passage, we will tend to hang on, not to the imagined elbow straps but to the thread of the continuing music and experience the 'exaltation' of Vernon Lee's 'listeners'. Both kinds of audition involve recognition of some elements of the presented schemata, but in one instance as rich abstract fusions of myriad past features; and in the other, as a kind of snap-shot, reminiscent only of a particular event. Speculative as such a theory may be, it is an attempt to answer the question of what the 'subject' of music may be, namely, the schema or dynamic properties of past experience. Incidentally, it already raises the issue of what music education is really about; which of these levels of concentration is our aim?

The relationship of posture and gesture with feeling and emotional states has been helpfully analysed by Charlotte Wolff (Wolff, 1945). Each gesture is, for Wolff, a 'synthesis of many movements' from a basic postural 'platform'. Fundamental gestures include those of forward drive and inhibition, reaching out and withdrawal. According to Wolff, the posture of a 'happy' person is characterized by 'roundness'. The 'flexor muscles become rounder through animated circulation and reinforced tone' (p. 9). There are striking unintentional resemblances between her descriptions of patterns of posture and gesture and the ways in which people say they hear music. It seems worth giving just a few examples here.

The state of *extreme inhibition*, Wolff tells us, is often characterized by extensor movements, withdrawal, stereotyped and arhythmical movements, motor unrest, slow motor speed and unnecessary movements. *Depression* may display itself in slow motor speed, non-emphatic gesture, hesitating, tightness of posture and very few unnecessary movements. *Elation* is shown by a wealth of unnecessary movement, fast motor speeds, exhibitionist behaviour, spontaneous, emphatic and rhythmical gesture and self-assertiveness. *Anxiety* is often revealed in unnecessary movement with 'perseverance', ambivalent motor speed, fidgeting and variable forward impulse. All of these descriptive terms can just as easily be applied to the character of music as to the symptoms of feeling states. For instance, we would be very unlikely to classify as 'exuberant and outgoing' a performance of music with a slow motor speed, non-emphatic gestures, full of hesitations and tension and repeated fidgeting little figures.

Even the way we walk signals a quality of feeling. It has been suggested that there are seven measurable attributes in gait: 'regularity, speed, pressure, length of stride, elasticity, definiteness of direction, and variability' (Allport and Vernon, 1935). Music is well-adapted to communicate particular kinds of forward motion. Terms like *giusto, ritmico, a tempo, pesante*, and *rubato* serve to point a few parallels, in a relationship recognized by many, including Jaques-Dalcroze.

> Rhythm, like dynamics, depends entirely on movement, and finds its nearest prototype in our muscular system. All the nuances of time — *allegro, andante, accelerando, ritenuto* — all the nuances of energy — *forte, piano, crescendo, diminuendo* — can be 'realized' by our bodies, and the acuteness of our musical feeling will depend on the acuteness of our bodily sensations.
>
> (Jaques-Dalcroze, 1921: 81)

There is experimental evidence to show that music can be described in terms of weight, size, stiffness, outward or inward direction and the degree of activity (Swanwick, 1971, 1973, 1979). Such descriptions were given at a statistically significant level by children as young as seven, in response to simple musical phrases. Correlations were found between crude emotional labels, for instance, 'sadness', and the more subtle postural qualities of heaviness, passivity and inward-lookingness. This is hardly surprising. We inevitably use postural metaphors by which to communicate the qualities of affective states. We all know what is meant when someone says that they were made to feel 'small', or were weighed down with care, stiff with fright, 'heavy' with apprehension, 'light as air', 'depressed', and so on. Nor are such expressions unique to the English language.

The expressive character of a musical passage is thus determined by our perception of its apparent weight, size, forward impulse, manner of movement and other components of posture and gesture. Since such constructs are formulated within the relativities of particular musical contexts; no analysis of physiological change or measurement of isolated aural abilities will help us to understand them. The metaphorical nature of such 'meanings' may account for the power of music to stir and move people, even when there may be no words, no 'programme', and no obvious association with particular cultural values. Metaphorical richness accounts for much of the affective charge of poetry, drama and literature: there is no reason to suppose that music is not also charged, all the more powerfully by being free from literalness of representation; being fluently *expressive* but not naturally *descriptive*.

Music that is heard as strongly characterized will, like meaningful words, be the more easily recalled or at least recognized. Music expressively neutralized, as is often the case in aural tests, will not haunt the mind for long. One experiment illustrates the point. Delis, Fleer and Kerr (1978) found that recognition of previously heard musical passages was superior when titles were given communicating a 'concrete' visual image as a basis for subjects to construct their own 'designative interpretations' of the musical extracts. They attribute this to the fact that memory is superior when people find the stimulus meaningful, as would also be the case if we were to try to memorize a list of real words rather than nonsense syllables. Although we may have reservations about the imposition of such titles, there is little doubt that the principle stands. We remember what is meaningful, something which becomes obvious if we give ourselves a few seconds to try to memorize these lists.

List 1	List 2
BOC	PIN
SIO	LIP
LEB	MIX
PEY	ONE
ABB	SIN
NIN	SEX

Musical structure

The ultimately distinguishing feature of musical individuality, originality and quality is not found at the level of inventing new sound materials or even in making expressive gestures, but in unique relationships brought about by musical speculation — the transformation of sound and gesture into musical structure. Unfortunately, the very word 'structure' tends to suggest a fixed *construction* and elicits images of strictly notated pieces or movements in 'sonata form'. Let us be clear: musical structure is simply the effectiveness with which one expressive gesture is heard to relate to another; this applies as much to an improvised jazz solo as to a movement of a symphony.

An influential and penetrating account of how musical structure can be seen as a dynamic process is given by Meyer (1956). Meyer accepts a psychological principle, that feeling, or affect, is most intense when reactions are stimulated 'that do not gain expression either in conduct, emotional expression, or fantasy' (MacCurdy, 1925). In Meyer's terms: 'Emotion or affect is aroused when a tendency to respond is arrested or inhibited'. He shows how, within a particular musical culture, expectancies are aroused which are fulfilled, delayed or inhibited. Incomplete musical figures set up a desire for completion; passing over a note without sounding it in a known scale series creates a need to hear that note; in the context of a style, unresolved chords have us waiting for resolution; and so on. From these observations, Meyer generates a theory which identifies important *cognitive* aspects of music, particularly the operation of stylistic norms against which deviations are perceived.

Such a theory owes rather more in fact to Gestalt psychology than to MacCurdy's theory of the emotions, and it is the Gestalt basis that is most helpful in describing the way in which music is structured and perceived. The fundamental act of perception is to see pattern, form or configuration. Perception is essentially the organization of sensory stimulation into meaningful wholes. Simply to survive, we 'theorize' about potentially confusing noises made up of pitch, timbre, duration and loudness; we impose tonality, we hear melodies, counterpoints, imitation, sequences, style; just as Lord Edward did in the passage at the head of this chapter. We learn to do this through experience of the world and especially through interaction — actually handling things for ourselves.

It is a universal human need to make *gestalten*, to see everything as form. Conversely, the human species has a strong tendency — also necessary for adaptation and survival — to break a mould, to violate a *gestalt*, to replace one configuration with another. Every good joke reveals this force at work as does every other act of originality, however small. Musical structure arises at once from our need to perceive coherent groupings and at the same time from the need to play imaginatively with new possibilities. When participating in music, we can become conscious of this tension. Hans Keller puts it thus:

The background of a composition is both the sum total of the
expectations a composer raises in the course of a piece without
fulfilling them, and the sum total of those unborn fulfilments.
The foreground is, simply, what he does instead — what is
actually in the score.

(Keller, 1970)

Gestalt processes involved in musical perception have been
described elsewhere, notably by Deutsch and Sloboda. We
distinguish 'figure' from 'ground' when we pick out a melodic line
from accompaniment or a rhythmic figure from a texture. We work
with 'closure', or completion, to help us to trace a melody that is
woven into guitar arpeggio figuration, hearing the line as continuous
although it may be only sketched in between other notes. Sounds
that are close together in time tend to be grouped on the basis of
'proximity', heard not as separate but as pairs or patterns. If sounds
become very spaced out, when, for instance music is excessively
slow, it becomes difficult to hear melodic line or rhythm patterns
and our grouping efforts fail. The organizing principle of 'similarity'
operates when we follow a particular instrumental or vocal timbre,
hanging on to the sound of a flute or a particular drum within a
texture. A further *gestalt* principle, that of 'good continuation', is
evident when, for example, a phrase shape is heard in sequential
repetition, although the register, instrumentation, and precise
intervallic relationships may all have changed. The 'sameness' of
a figure can still be recognized even if it only approximates to
previous appearances: the gesture may be modified or transformed
but the anticipated overall shape is not lost.

These processes are mentioned here only to show something of
the complexity of the listener's activity, who, unless merely
overhearing music, is bound to be generating a potential musical
future during the evolution of a work as it unfolds, on the basis
of sorting figure from ground, completing the incomplete, grouping the proximate and the similar and looking for some kind of
musical logic in continuity. I ought to emphasize that I include
composer, improviser and performer in the category of 'listener'.
Whatever role we take in relationship to music, the same fundamental psychological processes are at work. I hope it is clear by now
that I am concerned here with the 'listener' in Vernon Lee's use
of the term: someone who attends to music, and not to *something
else* while music takes place.

The *gestalt* perspective was anticipated over a hundred years ago by Hanslick, who, sounding very like Meyer and Keller, writes:

> The most important factor in the mental process which
> accompanies the act of listening to music, and which converts
> it into a source of pleasure, is frequently overlooked. We here
> refer to the intellectual satisfaction which the listener derives
> from continually following and anticipating the composer's
> intentions — now to see his expectation fulfilled, and now
> to find himself agreeably mistaken. It is a matter of course
> that this intellectual flux and reflux, this perceptual giving
> and receiving, takes place unconsciously and with the rapidity
> of lightning flashes.
>
> (Hanslick, 1854, 1957: 98)

Such engagement is impossible if an inadequate 'set' is brought
to the experience. Listening for motivic development in much
African drumming, for Wagner-like orchestration in Haydn, for
tonal tensions in modal plainsong, or for western scales in certain
Indian *ragas* would usually be inappropriate.

When we talk of effective musical structure we are really talking
of the organization of expressive gestures into a significant, cohesive,
engaging whole. It is not sound materials that are structured but
musical characterizations or gestures. The characterization itself
lays down a charge of feeling with which we to some extent empathize. And these feeling schema, these 'ghosts', are vitalized by
being combined in new and surprising relationships. Thus, effective music depends not only on *what* is expressed but that it should
be *well* expressed. Rewarding listening depends on the ability to
'go along' with particular expressive characterizations and, at the
same time, to feel what Bullough called aesthetic 'distance', to
recognize that a musical work, whether notated, remembered or
improvised, has a life of its own and will at times defy our predic-
tions and expectations. Music is indeed one of Popper's 'World
Three' inhabitants.

The ability — and it is a considerable ability — to make and
respond to music on these terms can only be nurtured and grow
from substantial musical experience. Some of this experience may
be acquired informally in society through the process of enculturation. Education — a more deliberate and usually more formal affair
— can help to amplify this development, facilitating psychological
access to music.

I have tried to extract from a selection of psychological literature some important themes that may help us to compose a coherent theory of music and music education. If we were to organize in summary the psychological strands that I have tried to tease out, they might look something like this:

MUSICAL RESPONSE

LEVELS	DISTRACTIONS
ATTENTION TO SOUND SOURCE	NOISE: unwanted sounds, discomfort, social setting, fatigue etc.
IMPRESSION OF SOUND MATERIALS	SOUND ASSOCIATION: similarities with other sounds, synaesthesia, labelling and classifications
PERCEPTION OF EXPRESSIVE CHARACTER	EXTRA-MUSICAL ASSOCIATION: dramatic or visual, emotional associations
STRUCTURAL FRAMING OF THE WORK	EXPECTATIONS: level of familiarity, mental 'set', sense of style
VALUE POSITION	DISSONANT SYSTEM: alternative peer-group affiliation, inappropriate location, contrary 'philosophy'

In subsequent chapters I shall say more about value positions. The next move, though, is to begin to assemble a unifying theory of music that puts these particular experiments and observations into perspective without violating our intuitions about what music really *is*. The way forward here is to come to music from a totally different angle, seeing it as one of those distinctive human activities we call the arts.

3

The arts, mind, and education

What we have not named
or beheld as a symbol
escapes our notice
             (From W.H. Auden's 'I am not a camera')

I take the risk here of sketching in what I think is a psychological
profile of the arts; how they contribute to the development of *mind*.

What is the point and purpose of the arts? Are they simply
pleasurable activities for private gratification or are they a form of
public discourse? Can they be handled in classrooms or are they
best enjoyed away from institutions? Is assessment in the arts rather
like grading a dream or children's play? Can we teach dreaming
or playing? What important purposes, if any, lie behind our
attempts to educate in and about the arts? Where lie the
psychological roots of the arts?

These are more than questions of justification, more than an
invitation to special pleading for time, resources and recognition.
For if we subscribe to an inadequate or false account of the *value* of
arts activities, we shall misunderstand what we are about in education and art, distorting the enterprise itself. Inevitably, curriculum
decisions, choice of classroom activities, teaching styles and modes
of assessment, depend upon the formulation and the tone of voice
of our answer to the question: 'Why the arts?', 'Why this art?'.

The value of the arts

The Gulbenkian Report, *The Arts in Schools*, helpfully assembles
before us a whole range of answers to the question of value

(Gulbenkian Foundation, 1982: 18-40). Here the arts are seen as distinct categories of understanding, special forms of thought; they give us a grasp of the 'growth and tenor of our civilization'; they are ways of having ideas, of bringing about new insights and illuminations; they provide a counterbalance to analytical forms of discourse, such as science and maths, and lead us towards synthesis and wholeness; they utilize the right hemisphere of the brain, with its propensity for dealing with the sensuous, intuitive and spatial elements of perception and action. The arts confer other benefits through the processes of transfer; they develop certain qualities and abilities such as poise, grace and co-ordination; they encourage 'discipline, dedication and attention to detail'; they aid interpersonal and even international understanding. Admirable as all this is, it still seems somewhat unsatisfactory. There are, perhaps, too many good reasons. This report is an illuminating and persuasive document, but it lacks a steady value-description based on a convincing account of the development of mind.

Unless the arts can be seen to develop mind (in the broadest sense), their function cannot ultimately be understood, nor can their role in education. Education is surely more than merely having 'experiences', or acquiring a repertoire of skills and facts. It has to do with developing understanding, insightfulness: qualities of mind.

Where the arts have been seriously taken into a view of mind, it has proved difficult to transcribe the complexities and range of argument into a working philosophy for education — I think here especially of the extensive and influential writings of Suzanne Langer and Louis Arnaud Reid. Thinking more specifically of education in schools, Robert Witkin and Malcolm Ross, have emphasized a 'creative self-expression' value position for the arts. Through artistic creation, it is claimed, we can recognize, order and externalize our disturbances, our feelings, thus resolving 'sensate difficulty'. This is undoubtedly part of the truth, though I have some problems with it. The theory is not able to deal convincingly with our response to art objects and events created by other people, nor does it account for why, during these encounters, we often feel 'stirred up', moved with feeling, disturbed — rather than either discharging or ordering emotions we may bring along with us. The implication is that the arts are highly personal, 'subjective', especially when compared with the more 'objective' sciences and humanities.

This relegation of the arts to a realm of private feeling, even if we call it 'subject-reflexive' action, is not retrieved by arguing that they are legitimate alternative modes of discourse, having their own special logic and intelligence. The break with cognitive processes and other acts of mind becomes hard to mend. However, I do not wish to denigrate the work of Witkin and Ross, and I am aware of the danger of oversimplifying their extensive and complex argument. They have been positively influential in communicating a strong sense of the importance of the arts in education.

The arts as 'different'

The separation of the arts from the main business of life and education is quite common. Herbert Spencer put forward the classic view in 1911, that, as the arts occupied the leisure part of life, they should occupy 'the leisure part of education (Spencer, 1911). More recently, investigation into the special functions of the right hemisphere of the brain has also emphasized the special functions of the sensuous, the spatial, the intuitive; perhaps the inarticulate? The arts are frequently seen as creating dream-worlds into which we can escape from 'reality'. Jean-Paul Sartre put it very strongly.

> Aesthetic contemplation is an induced dream and the passing into the real is an actual waking up. We often speak of the 'deception' experienced on returning to reality. But this does not explain that this discomfort also exists, for instance, after having witnessed a realistic and cruel play, in which case reality should be experienced as comforting. This discomfort is simply that of the dreamer on awakening; an entranced consciousness, engulfed in the imaginary, is suddenly freed by the sudden ending of the play, of the symphony, and come suddenly into contact with existence. Nothing more is needed to arouse the nauseating disgust that characterizes the consciousness of reality.
>
> (Sartre, 1950: 37)

In case this may appear to be merely one of the more negative symptoms of existential philosophy, consider the more moderate and analytical tone of Professor Peters:

> It might reasonably be argued that literature and poetry, for instance, are developments of a dimension of awareness of

37

the world, while the other arts, like music, may be creating, as it were, another world to be aware of.

(Peters, 1966: 160)

Richard Peters speculates that the non-verbal arts may be like games, in creating these other 'worlds' that are somehow different from '*the* world', presumably the 'real' world. The implication is clear: some of the arts, at least, are dreamlike, or, at least, 'playlike', they are 'other-worldly'.

The connection between dreaming, day-dreaming, and play is well made. Freud tells us that the 'opposite of play is not what is serious but what is real', and observes that as people grow up they cease to play and *seem* to give up the pleasure derived from playing. And he goes on:

Actually, we can never give anything up; we only exchange one thing for another . . . . In the same way, the growing child, when he stops playing, gives up nothing but the link with real objects; instead of playing, he now *phantasizes*. He builds castles in the air and creates what are called *day-dreams*.

(Freud, 1908, in Vernon, 1970: 126–35)

Freud closely identifies one art, the art of literature, with play and with fantasy, with day-dreams: 'The creative writer does the same as the child at play. He creates a world of phantasy which he takes very seriously.'

This idea of the unreality of play is quite general. Vygotsky notes the clear separation of play from 'real life', 'the first effect of the child's emancipation from situational constraints'. He defines imagination — a word much used in connection with the arts — as 'play without action' (Vygotsky, 1976: 537–54). We too might notice the linguistic relationship between the word play and the practice of the arts. We *play* music; we go to the theatre to see a *play*; a cunning rhyme may be a *play* on words. Such usage is not confined to the English language and can be found, for example, in German *spielen* and French *jouer*.

The question remains: while we would all recognize the importance to us all of dreaming, playing *and* art, and the seriousness which characterizes these phenomena, are schools appropriate places for *any* of these things and, if so, how can they be taught? It is not my mission to argue the case for dreaming or play in the curriculum though there is a case to be made for the arts. This issue is not only to do with curriculum justification, but rather of educational explanation, trying to clarify the nature of the task of teachers involved in arts education.

The arts as dreaming

Although there are apparent similarities, there are also crucial differences between dreaming and artistic activity. Freud regarded the interpretation of dreams as 'the royal road to a knowledge of the unconscious activities of the mind' (Freud, 1953: 66). For Freud, dreams are essentially wish-fulfilments, though these wishes are usually disguised to enable them to pass through the 'censor' part of mind. A dream, for Freud, has a 'manifest content', the details which we actually remember; the substance of the dream; and a 'latent content', that hidden substance which gives the dream its meaning, often to do with death or sexuality. What Freud calls the 'dreamwork' consists of the process by which the latent content, the hidden message, becomes transformed into the manifest content, the dream itself that we can describe in the morning.

To what extent then is this dreamwork similar to artwork? The dreamwork is supposed to involve at least three processes: *condensation*, the reduction of detail by generalization; *displacement*, the way in which the latent content is disguised; the *representation*, or the attempt to maintain a consistent imagery. We know from recalling our dreams just how difficult it is to keep the displaced images consistent, and how illogical and silly dreams can appear to be. Certainly we can recognize the process of condensation: it is surprising just how packed with references a brief dream may be — as when in a dream I sometimes have, rooms from several houses in which I happen to have lived are brought together in one dream house.

Let us take an art work — a poem is easiest under the circumstances of the printed word — and see if these dream processes can be identified. Here are the first fourteen lines of Wilfred Owen's 'The parable of the old man and the young' (Owen, 1920: 42):

So Abram rose, and clave the wood, and went,
And took the fire with him and a knife.
And as they sojourned both of them together,
Isaac the first-born spake and said, My Father,
Behold the preparations, fire and iron,
But where the lamb for this burnt-offering?

Then Abram bound the youth with belts and straps,
And builded parapets and trenches there,
And stretched forth the knife to slay his son.
When lo! an angel called him out of heaven,
Saying, Lay not thy hand upon the lad,
Neither do anything to him. Behold,
A ram, caught in a thicket by its horns;
Offer the Ram of Pride instead of him. . . .

Here we certainly have tremendous condensation, a dramatic Old
Testament story reduced to a few compressed lines, yet retaining
archaic words; 'clave', 'first-born', 'behold', 'lo'. And this story
undergoes a kind of displacement; it runs alongside other images:
belts, straps, parapets, trenches, fire and iron; images from the First
World War. But this is *not* a dream; one set of images is not just
a substitute or disguise for another. We are invited to attend to both
at the same time. The poem is an extended and cohesive metaphor,
deliberately wrought and consciously explored; it has an almost
ruthless *consistency* of image.

Freud regarded the main purpose of dreams to be '*the guardians
of sleep*'. Noises in the night, internal physiological changes, loose
worries from the day: all tend to be incorporated into dreams to
keep us from waking up. The dreamwork attempts to hold startling
things at bay, and if it does not succeed then we may experience
unpleasant effects — nightmares — and wake up 'in a state'. For
example, we may fall out of bed and dream that we are falling — a
desperate attempt to stay asleep — eventually becoming uncomfort-
able enough to wake up, to discover that we are on the floor. What
happens if we read the Owen poem complete with the last two lines
and ask the direct question: is this work a 'guardian of sleep'?

But the old man would not so, but slew his son,
And half the seed of Europe, one by one.

We are surely disturbed, challenged, *woken up* by this accumulated
web of interlocking metaphor, by the sudden gathering of speed
and image, culminating with a painful structural twist in the final
lines, which are full of historical, political and human implications.
This is not the *anaesthetic* experience of sleep, but the *aesthetic* experience of art. We come to perceive, to feel *more*, not less. We are not
held in sleep but pushed towards heightened awareness, greater
consciousness.

It would obviously be easy to cite other examples to support this view, from literature, drama, or from dance and the visual arts, when they are obviously representational. But what of music and so-called abstract art?

As I tried to show in the previous chapter, even music, though abstract to a high degree, is essentially metaphorical, and can raise before us *images* — perhaps of hard edges, or of throbbing movement, of fleeting shadows, of massive substance, or of flowing tranquility — and relate these in logically evolving structures that rise before us with the same ordered and sequential presence as poems and plays. How different from dreaming, with its disguised meanings, its dislocated and inconsistent imagery, and its soporific mission.

Even so, there may still be a strange sense of disquiet or, at least, of disturbance when moving back from art to 'life'. There is *something* different about art experiences that sets them apart from other things. I want to return to this sense of 'unreality' in a while, but for the moment, move from setting art against dreams to examine the possibly more directly relevant concept of play.

The arts as play

Play is more easily controlled than dreams, but it shares with dreaming several features: objects may stand in for other objects — 'this clothes-peg is really a soldier'; there is wish-fulfilment — 'I'll be Superman this time'; there is conversion of fearful situations into security by stylized repetition — pretending to be doctors, dentists, or teachers. Play in very early childhood is characterized especially by the pleasure of mastery, what Piaget calls 'a feeling of virtuosity or power' (Piaget, 1951: 87–9). I think of the pleasure babies get from throwing a toy out of a pram over and over again, just enjoying the experience of control; or the two-year-old who has just managed to climb steps, trekking up and down repeatedly for the sheer sense of achievement.

Play soon becomes imaginative and 'subjects things to the child's activity, without rules or limitations'. This, says Piaget, is pure *assimilation*, 'though polarized by preoccupation with individual satisfaction, where children seem actually to think that their 'make-believe' world really exists. At one time, I was accompanied on walks not only by three children but also by a horse, which, though completely invisible, was something of a nuisance, causing us to open gates rather than climb stiles and making us wait while it was

41

fed. This enigmatic animal was a fairly constant companion for several months, a vividly imagined being.

Pretending to *have* a horse is very different from pretending to *be* one. That would be an instance of yet another crucial element of play, evident from the first year of life. Piaget calls it *imitation*, the process of *accommodation*, and regards it as the opposite of imaginative play. When imitating, the child accommodates him or her self to the impression of external objects, people and events, taking over some of their characteristics and, to some extent, becoming like them; pretending to be an animal or whatever. In imaginative play, the world around us is transformed to our standards: in imitation, we are transformed, we become like something else.

In the succeeding chapters, I shall show how making and responding to music depends upon these three play impulses. For now, I shall draw attention to the essentials of the relationships between the arts and these three elements.

Mastery, imitation and imaginative play

We can relate to art in one of three ways: as a *former* (composer, improviser, painter, choreographer, poet); as a *performer* (executant musician, actor, dancer, public reader of poetry); *in audience* (art gallery, concert hall, private reading, listening, looking). In the case of improvised art the roles of former and performer may seem to be fused. However, there are nearly always decisions to be made about the way the event is to be presented to others — such considerations as programme order — quite distinct from the improvisation itself. In the case of the visual arts, forming and performing co-exist in a totally fused way, though even there may be presentational decisions to make, such as those relating to the mounting of an exhibition or writing a guide or introduction.

Each of these modes tends to have its own main bias among the play elements. *Forming*, 'doing your own thing', may have about it a strong feeling of assimilation, of imaginative play; creating something to satisfy our own internal specifications. Being *in audience* would certainly require us to accommodate to the object or event: if we respond sympathetically we are, to some extent, internally imitating, empathizing with its gestures. If we dance or move to music, the imitation is quite apparent. In the audience role, we are bound to feel to some extent as the work appears to us; perhaps caught up in a fast flow of words or gestures, identifying with a character, or feeling to some extent the quality of a particular visual impression; whether still or moving, heavy or freeflowing. In *performance*, along with this leaning towards imitative empathy with the work, there may also be a bias towards the play element of mastery, towards the enjoyment of 'virtuosity'.

Sometimes, arts education appears to proceed in a partial or lopsided manner. The teaching of music has, until relatively recently, tended to exclude genuine elements of imaginative play (forming, composition, improvisation), and instead has focused on the mastery of performance skills and 'appreciation', or listening to music in audience, both of which are essentially imitative in emphasis. Visual art education seemed to move long ago towards imaginative play, in the sense that students make their own art and may have played down the element of imitation in the educational process that arises through attention to the work of others. I suspect that in dance there is a strong pull towards the element of mastery in performance, while in drama education, one of the important issues seems to be the extent to which imitation should be predominant in the guise of role-play.

There is, however, a much more direct correspondence with the arts and this analysis of play, a relationship which bears upon day-to-day classroom objectives and activities. In particular, I think of three types of problem which students may be asked to solve, or three starting points for any curriculum session or project. Each of these corresponds strongly with one play element: mastery; imitation; imaginative play.

Mastery

It is possible to focus on the materials of a particular art: colours, duration, tones, words, gestures, and so on. Handling materials inevitably involves mastery of some skill, fluency with words or movements, ability with instruments, notations, brushes, knives and so on. So we may select and become sensitive to these materials coming to control them. For example, we may work with or notice the use of black and white, hard and soft, movements that are smooth or movements that are angular. In music, the prescription of sets of sound materials has always been an obvious feature of compositional processes. It seems essential for composers to limit available resources, in order to make music manageable and get them started. Thus we have the tonal system, 12-note techniques,

pentatonic scales, Indian *ragas*, and more limited sets of sound —
as we find when Debussy makes a piano prelude out of the interval
of the third, or when Bartók writes pieces in his *Mikrokosmos* based
on 'fifth chords', or 'triplets in 9/8 time', or when jazz musicians
improvise on the harmonic foundation of a well-known 'standard'
tune, or a blues chord sequence. Colleagues in the other arts will
easily think of parallels, I am sure.

Sets of materials are educationally invaluable in extending
techniques, in sharpening discriminations, and in emphasizing
particular relationships. Mastery may involve manipulative skills,
perceptual judgements and discriminations, and, at times, handling
notations in the form of scores, scripts, plans, and so on. I am not
thinking merely of 'exercises', but of ways in which we can actually
get going in the arts. Nor does this analysis relate only to forming
and performing. The spectator or listener may also focus on
materials and techniques and become caught up in the way that
certain colours, tones, techniques are handled. Just how does a
painter achieve this or that effect? What types of sound give this
music its character? We can also admire sheer virtuosity for its own
sake.

Imitation

The more obviously representational an arts activity is, the more
it refers to events in life; the more it is imitative, having what I
call *expressive character*. Teachers frequently take imitation as a focus
for classroom or studio work. Thus, in drama we might initiate role-
playing, acting *like* someone else. In literature we might tell a story
from another's point of view. In the visual arts we might try to represent a particular incident or person; or, in a more abstract way,
seek to render an impression, a feeling, a quality of experience.
In dance and music we might set the problem of communicating
a particular dynamic process; the coming of darkness, or dawn,
the gesture of shrivelling up or of opening out, a sense of increasing
stillness or activity. Though these imitative judgements are most
apparent in the process of *forming*, yet, in the performance of written
music, or in the theatre, there is still scope for the player to make
decisions about the detailed expression of the work, to take an active
part in shaping the imitation, determining to some extent the
expressive character. Only in larger and more mechanized performances — huge orchestras, bands, pageants — is there a necessity

to work almost entirely 'by numbers', and not make decisions about expressive character.

Imitation is not mere copying, but includes sympathy, empathy, identification with, concern for, seeing ourselves as something or someone else. It is the activity by which we enlarge our repertoire of action and thought. No meaningful art lacks references, by imitation, to things outside of itself. Imitation is as inevitable as delight in the mastery of materials and is certainly not hostile to creative imagination.

Imaginative play

If mastery is the element of play that directs us towards the materials of art and if imitation relates to the expressive, or referential character of art, then imaginative play would have us focus on the *structure* of art. As I tried to make clear in the previous chapter, by structure I mean bringing things into relationships; tendencies that can lead us on expectantly or be broken off to surprise and delight us. Freud tells this little story:

> The Prince, travelling through his domain, noticed a man in the cheering crowd who bore a striking resemblance to himself. He beckoned him over and asked: 'Was your mother ever employed in my palace?'
> 'No, Sire' the man replied. 'But my father was.'
> (Cited in Koestler, 1964: 66)

Here our expectations to do with the relationship of King to commoner are turned right around, within a further relationship to certain norms of sexual behaviour. As Wollheim says, in humour 'a moment's mobility is granted to the mind' (Wollheim, 1971: 105). There is more than a superficial similarity between the 'punchline' device in this story and the arresting conclusion to the poem by Wilfred Owen.

In art, these relationships can evolve at times into such powerful perseverant structures that we cannot imagine the world without them. To give just the start of a personal list: a planet on which there was no *First Symphony* by Sibelius, no *Pietà* or *Firebird*, no *Magic Mountain*, no *Graceland*, none of the smaller gems of folk and popular art, would be a bare, inhospitable landscape.

In the classroom, working with structure is perhaps the most difficult and sophisticated task. At the very simplest level, structure depends on recognizable repetitions and contrasts. How is this melody, or dramatic character, or passage of description, or set of dance movements different from that? Is the change gradual or sudden? How does it change? Beyond this we cannot go without invoking imitation, invoking expressive character. What *kind* of change is it? Does it become more or less agitated, calmer, warmer, lighter, less or more aggressive? We also become curious about mastery of the materials. How is the change brought about? What is being manipulated, controlled, to bring about this effect?

My suggestion here is simply that all three elements of play will be activated in arts education, at all ages. It may be helpful to begin with a problem of mastery, or character, or structure, but once an activity is underway we shall be looking for a strong interaction between them; for how can we have any real experience of art without some level of mastery and some response to the elements of imitation and imaginative play?

The arts and the intellect

So what? There may be fun in the play elements of the arts, but do they contribute to the development of *mind*, or must we say with Cardinal Newman:

> stuffing birds or playing stringed instruments is an elegant
> pastime, and a resource to the idle, but it is not education;
> it does not form or cultivate the intellect.
>
> (Newman, 1915: 136–7)

The answer to this can be begun only if we broaden our notion of mind and intellect, liberating ourselves from any rigid correlation of thought with verbal language.

> Now, in a convulsion of the understanding Lok found himself
> using likeness as a tool as surely as ever he had used a stone
> to hack at sticks or meat. Likeness could grasp the white-faced
> hunters with a hand, could put them into the world where
> they were thinkable and not a random and unrelated
> irruption.
>
> (Golding, 1959: 194)

What is interesting here is the absence of words; yet the world is
still 'thinkable' through metaphor, through 'likeness'. Einstein
attempts to describe the process:

> The words or the language, as they are written or spoken,
> do not seem to play any role in any mechanism of thought.
> The physical entities which seem to serve as elements in
> thought are certain signs and more or less clear images which
> can be 'voluntarily' reproduced or combined . . . . But taken
> from a psychological viewpoint, this combinatory play seems
> to be the essential feature in productive thought — before
> there is any connection with logical construction in words or
> other kinds of signs which can be communicated to others.
> The above-mentioned elements are, in my case, of visual and
> some of muscular type. Conventional words or other signs
> have to be sought for laboriously only in a secondary stage,
> when mentioned associative play is sufficiently established and
> can be reproduced at will.
>
> (Cited by Eisner, 1980: 13)

It would be inappropriate here to trawl the literature on language
and thought. It will suffice to say that the theory that all thinking
is done with words having designated meaning is not one that bears
much weight. There are layers of thought and consciousness where
the real work is done before and during verbal articulation. Iris
Murdoch puts it this way:

> Each human being swims within a sea of faint suggestive
> imagery. It is this web of pressures, currents and suggestions,
> something often so much less definite than pictures, which
> ties our fugitive present to our past and future, composing
> a globe of consciousness. We think with our body, with its
> yearning and shrinkings and its ghostly walkings.
>
> (Murdoch, cited by Abbs, 1982)

Several of the arts have little if anything to do with words. When
words are part of the material of an art work they have more than
denotative, literal meanings. But we should not be satisfied with
any suggestion that the arts are merely pre-verbal or sub-verbal.
They are *supra-verbal*: fully-flowering systems of precise and richly
articulated forms, requiring layers of experience and insight if we
are to understand them. Just because some of the arts — music, the

visual arts, and dance especially — are essentially non-verbal and apparently easily enjoyed, we ought not to assume that they necessarily have a low level of cognitive content, that they can function only at the level of the sensori-motor and cannot stimulate what Piaget calls 'conceptual intelligence'. We may agree with Einstein and Iris Murdoch and also with Polanyi, that 'we can know more than we can tell' (Polanyi, 1967). There are, though, other ways of 'telling' besides verbal language. The arts as ways of knowing are as potentially powerful as any other form of human discourse, and they are just as capable of contributing to the development of mind on a conceptual level. Of course, there are lower levels of operation, where wish-fulfilment and fantasy are prime: but the same is true of language itself. It does not always serve the upper reaches of intelligence and the higher realms of sensitivity. Consult any newpaper stand; eavesdrop on committee meetings; listen to many politicians.

How then does sensori-motor intelligence, thinking 'with the body', develop into 'conceptual intelligence'. How does our intuitively physical and practical way of taking the world, the 'intelligence of situations', evolve into more abstract, and therefore more flexible ways of thinking? Piaget has an explanation and specifies four conditions for this development (Piaget, 1951: 238-9).

1. We find ways of internally representing actions to ourselves, instead of actually having to *do* them (we form images of running down a stream, leaping over it and balancing ourselves). This speeds up the action.
2. We recognize relationships between these internalized actions (we run, *then* leap, *then* balance). A certain series here can be reversed in thought.
3. We supply a system of signs — such as language (we have a vocabulary: 'run', 'leap', 'balance').
4. We share our thinking in a community of minds. You can experience something of my thoughts.

These processes characterize the arts just as much as philosophic discourse, scientific reasoning, or mathematical thinking. When painting a picture, composing music, refining a poem or evolving a dance; we are, through the process of imitation, taking actions and turning them into *images*; we sequence them in relationships; we work to a system of signs; of words, meaningful gestures, expressive textures and shapes, *and* we offer them up into a community of other minds. The arts can exert as much intellectual force as any other mode of symbol-making; they are part of Popper's'World Three'.

I am not suggesting that some sort of transfer is involved, that engaging in the arts improves reasoning skills, mathematical or scientific ability or what is sometimes called general intelligence. I just do not know whether or not this is the case. What I am certain of is that we can come to know and develop our knowing through artistic engagement and that the fundamental processes of mind are similar to those in other forms of discourse. It would be very odd if, say, musical or dramatic functioning were totally separate processes, either from each other or from, say, philosophizing or calculating: nature is not usually so wasteful as to prohibit borrowing from one system to another. There may be different frames of mind, as Gardner suggests, but mind at a deeper level is a unity, unique in each individual (Gardner, 1984). What is more, particularly creative people seem to have the ability to draw on several aspects of their experience, bringing together things that were previously not seen to be related, just as Wilfred Owen does in his poem.

Having so ambitiously — some will say dangerously — pushed out the boat, it remains to pull towards the destination of some implications. To do this I turn again to Piaget in *Play, Dreams and Imitation*, for in this book he comes closest to the concerns of art educators. He tells us that even the development of sensori-motor intelligence arises only when there is *an equilibrium between assimilation and accommodation*, a balance between imaginative play and imitation (p.5). To develop mind we need to convert the world to our own terms in imaginative ways but also, *at the same time*, re-adjust to external events.

In children, a lack of equilibrium can be charming; in adults it is more worrying, even in the direction of imaginative play. There is a classic story of a man who was observed by a policeman to be pulling along a brick, tied to a string. Because he was a 'community' policeman, he stopped to have a friendly word. 'That's a nice dog you have there; do you have a licence for it?' 'Don't be silly officer,' said the man, 'this isn't a dog, it's a brick.' 'Oh, sorry Sir,' said the constable, and went away looking puzzled. The man bent down to the brick and whispered, 'That was a narrow escape, Rover.'

Educators, concerned with the growth of mind, have to resist the purely imaginative and the exclusively imitative. Arts experiences unite both elements together in a dynamic equilibrium.

The ultimate value of the arts

I am trying to convey something of why people value the arts and why they are important in education. They are not very much like dreaming, more like play. They are unique activities where mastery, imitation and imagination can be deliberately sustained and amplified through and beyond childhood, unlike overt play which tends to disappear. The arts are, and have always been, essential for developing and sustaining mind, as are other forms of representation, including language. And this development of mind is *intrinsically* rewarding, absorbing, exciting. I.A. Richards puts it well in *Principles of Literary Criticism*:

> Everybody knows the feeling of freedom, of relief, of increased competence and sanity that follows any reading in which more than usual order and coherence has been given to our responses. We seem to feel that our command of life, our insight into it and our discrimination of its possibilities, is enhanced . . .
>
> (Richards, 1960: 185)

Unfortunately we tend to have those experiences rarely. Less ambitiously, E.M. Forster tells us that the arts 'deposit a grain of strength' in the mind (Forster, 1936, 1967: 85–9).

Although the arts have this characteristic in common with other human activities, it is the *special* function of art, to strengthen, to extend, to illuminate, to transform, and, ultimately, to make life worth living, more 'like life'. The subject of the arts is human consciousness, deliberately extended and explored. This is why art has been often linked with dreaming or 'other-worldliness'. Art intensifies, draws together, gives us not the confusion of mere experience, but what Dewey calls 'an experience' (Dewey, 1934). When it is over, of *course* we feel a dislocation, a jolt, a coming-to in another world, not because the world of art is less real but because it is *more* real, more vividly experienced, more alive, more highly integrated and structured than most of our existence. What we experience is a sense of loss, a kind of waking up to *less* reality, familiar to every child who does not want to finish the last page of a story.

Perhaps arts educators have not always grasped the psychological realities of their task, and have been persuaded by Cardinal Newman, administrators, politicians, and even students themselves, that the arts are 'pastimes', leisure activities, subjective experiences, non-essential, an elaborate form of day-dreaming, unreal. There is an element of truth in this: as we have seen, a flavour of 'other-worldliness' pervades the arts. But let us not confuse 'real' with dreary, with narrow, limited, pedestrian, or unimaginative, or with the limited perspective of one time and place. Each act of creativity in any sphere has about it a playful air. The arts are strongly adapted to this playful characteristic. Because of their highly sensual attractiveness, their imitative power and their imaginative possibilities, they are a significantly valued human activity, celebrated in every culture.

Tolkien was once asked if his epic story, *The Lord of the Rings*, was not unreal, not escapism. His reply was, 'Yes it is — escape from prison.'

4

Musical development: the early years

Daniel has one month to go before his third birthday. 'Can I come and stay with you', he says, 'you've got nice things in your house — a pano [piano] and a tar [guitar]'.

A frequent visitor, he makes himself at home with toys and has a fairly delicate improvisation on the piano. Then he asks for the guitar, which has been put away. He sits himself on a little stool and manages to hold the instrument in more or less the orthodox position, though it is rather big for him. He has handled it before and seen people play, both at home and on television, and he knows what it is to hold a guitar.

As usual, he strums with his thumb across the open strings, occasionally putting his ear to the body of the instrument and over the sound hole to listen to the dying resonances. He also draws his thumb across at different speeds, sometimes gently, sometimes striking the strings and throwing his right arm up into the air; a dramatic gesture which, we wonder, he might have seen guitarists do.

I show him how to pick single notes but he does this only once before reverting to strumming. Next time he plays the guitar he will make a point of picking it more often, telling me to listen to the different sound. Sometimes he sings snatches of songs he knows to this accompaniment, but this always gives way to the delight of the different sounds, to the pleasure of the actual vibration of the instrument and the special feeling of holding it; a sensation which he deliberately reactivates by putting it down and picking it up several times, moving from the stool to a chair with it as though beginning to play all over again.

After a while, I put on a disc of Julian Bream playing

Granados. Daniel sits spellbound for several minutes, sometimes briefly and gently joining in by lightly strumming his guitar, but mostly just listening, soaking up the sounds.

The concept of development

Everyday observation tells us that children develop as they grow older and that this development depends on an interaction between the genetic inheritance of each individual and the environment — the physical world, home, school, society. A second 'commonsense' observation is that there is an element of predictability about this process of development. We learn to walk before we can run, to stand up before we can do either, to imitate before we utter original statements, we become capable of sexual reproduction only when adolescence is reached. Of course, each person imposes his or her own style on these developmental sequences, but that there is development and that there are at least broad patterns of development are facts beyond dispute. Furthermore, it seems important, especially for teachers and parents, to have some understanding of these processes and to have a realistic set of expectations that correspond to the unfolding maturation of children in their care. The trouble is, in music education we seem very hazy about what to expect.

The psychologist, Eleanor Maccoby, tells us that we should distinguish between two general meanings of the term development. The first, which she calls the 'softer' definition, is the idea of sequential pattern; that development will occur usually in a certain order, that 'early behavioural acquisitions are necessary, though not sufficient, for later steps to occur'. The second definition 'goes beyond sequence', and predicates 'broad developmental changes that occur in almost all children according to a fairly standard timetable' (Maccoby, 1984). In other words, we could accept the idea of a series of progressive development, even if we had doubts about the timing of this in respect of individual children.

I want to suggest that there is a sequence, an orderly unfolding of *musical* behaviour, that there are cumulative stages through which the musical behaviour of children can be traced. It would be unwise to be too dogmatic about identifying broad developmental changes to a fairly standard timetable, especially to generalize this to 'almost *all* children'. However, this possibility is not ruled out and we have found several writers who, from quite different perspectives, seem to support such a view.

A good deal of research on the musical development of children has taken place in the USA. I do not wish to review this here, a job well done by Hargreaves (1986). In general, I am worried by the conceptual flavour of much of this work, which appears to be trying to approximate musical experience and musical development to developmental models generated with respect to other activities, such as maths. This has resulted in further testing for musical 'abilities', though of a different order from those pre-supposed by the earlier ability testers.

One outstanding example of this newer conception of musical abilities is the research of Marilyn Pflederer Zimmerman into musical 'conservation', linked as it is to experiments by Piaget into children's ability to recognize, for instance, that the volume of fluid remains the same even if it is transferred to a differently shaped beaker (Pflederer and Sechrest, 1968). As I indicated in the previous chapter, at a deep level, the fundamental operations of mind may indeed be similar. With Hargreaves, I remain to be convinced that the concept of conservation is on such a level, which is why I prefer to go further back into the theories of Piaget, to his ideas on play rather than his detailed analysis of the structure of scientific thinking (Hargreaves, 1986). In any case, observing children's more spontaneous musical behaviour is likely to tell us much more than the more limited activity of testing will allow.

An influential description of findings from observational techniques is the classic text by Helmut Moog, *The Musical Experience of the Pre-School Child*, which, though it has by definition little to say about the school-age child, is rich in detail as far as the very early years are concerned (Moog, 1976). In Britain, an example of the study of the musical products of children is to be found in Loane (1984b). He analyses the compositions of 11- to 14-year-olds and he views these in terms of a theoretical model based on the ideas of Langer: that music is a way of knowing the life of feeling. This sensitive and subtle approach to compositions of children illustrates not only the value of observation — in this case product evaluation — but also the virtue of declaring a conceptual framework. Without such organizing principles, any account of musical development in children will be merely descriptive, lacking both in interpretative interest and predictive power.

The theoretical basis

My own theoretical basis has already been partially laid. It centres on the idea that play, a vital human characteristic, is intrinsically bound up with all artistic activity; the early and obviously playful activities of early childhood being sublimated into activities such as painting pictures, playing music, making and performing plays and reading novels. A powerful influence in the development of this theory is certainly Piaget, though not the Piaget of tightly formulated and age-related stages of development but the Piaget who is concerned with fundamental human processes, those ways in which we make sense of and grow into the world.

Piaget, as we saw earlier, notes that play in early childhood is characterized by the sheer pleasure of exploring and mastering the environment, what he calls 'a feeling of virtuosity or power' (Piaget, 1951). This impulse towards mastery affects musical activities. The handling of voices and instruments; the development of ensemble skills; where appropriate, the use of notations; delight in the virtuosity of others: these are obvious elements of mastery. There is surely a developmental continuum of mastery from the pleasure experienced by a baby who has just learned to repeat a vocal sound or to shake a rattle continuously, to the achievement of a sitar player technically exploiting the potential of a particular *raga*.

Control of musical materials pre-supposes a degree of *delight* in the sounds themselves. Grieg in his later years, recalled his great excitement when, as a boy of six, he discovered for himself the chord of the ninth (Grieg, 1905). This piling up of thirds, one on top of the other, was an impressive sonorous phenomenon, yielding a delight which, at that stage, had little to do with musical expressive gestures or with structural ordering. Later on, this particular chord becomes a striking feature of his compositional style, as in, for example, his *Notturno* for piano.

Similarly, delight in sound materials as independent entities is described by Kenneth Grahame, the author of *The Wind in the Willows*, as he writes about the childhood experience of 'strumming' at the piano — much better than 'beastly exercises'.

Those who painfully and with bleeding feet have scaled the crags of mastery over musical instruments have yet their loss in this: that the wild joy of strumming has become a vanished sense. Their happiness comes from the concord and the relative value of the notes they handle; the pure, absolute

quality and nature of each note in itself are only appreciated
by the strummer . . . . And throughout all the sequence of
suggestion, up above the little white men leap and peep and
strive against the imprisoning wires.

(Grahame, 1885: 75)

At the start of this chapter, I described the relationship of Daniel
with his guitar. In just the same way as Grieg and Grahame, he
is responding primarily to the impressiveness of sound — the feel
of the instrument, the buzzing strings, the dying resonance.

Many composers of this century have attempted to return to this
state of childhood grace, starting afresh from sound itself in an
attempt to open up new musical possibilities. Take, for instance,
Stockhausen's advice to potential performers of *Gold Dust*, from *Aus
den Sieben Tagen*.

> for small ensemble
> GOLD DUST
> live completely alone for four days
> without food
> in complete silence, without much movement
> sleep as little as possible
> after four days, late at night
> without conversation beforehand
> play single sounds
> WITHOUT THINKING which you are playing
> close your eyes
> just listen

The following anecdote from Armenia is but one example from Peter
Hamel's account of the mystical and magical potential of sound;
sound not yet made into music but contemplated for itself, linked
with the belief that such meditation leads to insights and
enlightenment.

> An Armenian folk story tells of a man who played the 'cello.
> Every day he sat, playing the same note, hour after hour. His
> wife asked him why he did not do as other 'cellists, move his
> fingers up and down the strings to make other notes. He
> replied, they are looking for their note, I have found mine.
>
> (adapted from Hamel, 1976)

These illustrations remind us of the primordial power of music but they also raise musical and educational issues. What do we think about getting stuck on one note? Is such a minimalist attitude to music a form of arrested development? We all might give different answers: my own view is that a musical and educational philosophy that takes into account *only* this facet of human psychology is simply inadequate as a theory, as a basis for practice. It fails to nourish other vital aspects of mind. In particular, by limiting concentration on the impressiveness of experienced sound, it denies another natural desire, to *master* 'the crags' of musical materials, to manipulate instruments, to control as well as to savour sound. There are also *imitative* and *imaginative* elements in the repertoire of human mind, which are part of the very fibre of the arts and therefore of education in any art.

I have already described these elements in the previous chapter but feel it necessary to revisit them here briefly before considering children's musical development more systematically. Imitation is more obviously present in the arts when they are representational; that is to say, when there is reference to events in life — in stories and drama, in poems and paintings. Imitation is obvious enough in programme music and in opera but even in the most 'abstract' musical works there are essential imitative gestures. Every performance of a Bach fugue has its own particular universe of gestures, of feeling and emphasis; it has *expressive character*. Musical characterization is a direct development of the 'let's pretend' quality of imitation in early childhood. Fundamentally, and in Piaget's terminology, imitation — expressiveness in music — is an act of accommodation: to some extent we become like the music, taking on a trace of its feeling qualities, identifying with its postural and gestural *schema*.

Conversely, anyone who has observed children closely will know about the assimilative nature of imaginative play, where objects, events and people are transformed into other than themselves; where things are frequently conjured out of the air. In imaginative play we create a world of new relationships out of the elements around us. A new realm is created in a musical composition. For example, although the musical vocabulary and the expressive gestures of Mozart might often be fairly commonplace, 'of their time', they are transformed by the creation of new relationships on all levels. Musically speaking, imaginative play has to do with structural transformations, with the novel re-constitution of musical possibilities.

Figure 1 is a reminder of the relationships between the psychological concepts of *mastery*, *imitation*, and *imaginative play*, and their analogous musical elements: control of sound, expressive character and structure.

Figure 1: Play and the three elements of music

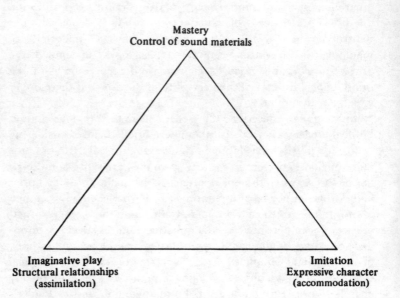

Mastery
Control of sound materials

Imaginative play
Structural relationships
(assimilation)

Imitation
Expressive character
(accommodation)

This theoretical starting point allows us to interpret the musical products of children in a developmental way. The musical compositions of children can be seen to follow a broad sequence of development through mastery, imitation and imaginative play, in that order.

Moog observed the beginnings of this process with six-month-old babies, where 'attention is given first and foremost to the sound itself'. He refers to other researchers who support this view, especially Mursell.

There are strong reasons for believing that a young child's

primary responsiveness to music is first and foremost the
tone itself, and not, as is sometimes asserted without any
good evidence, to rhythm or to melody.

(Mursell, 1948: 30)

Mursell is prepared to emphasize this point, stating that 'during
the pre-school and even the kindergarten period, the child is much
more pre-occupied with the tonal content and appeal of music than
with anything else about it.'

Moog's observations of young children lead him to the conclusion
that 'during the second year it is still the sensory impression of the
sound, together with the rhythm, which lie at the heart of musical
experience' (p.86). He also observes that before the age of one year
the songs of children bear 'no resemblance to what is sung or played
to them' (p.62). A good deal of what Moog calls musical babbling
goes on, clearly related to the fascination of sound itself and the
pleasure of beginning to control sound. After the age of one, children
begin to demonstrate the skill of reproducing what they hear, a form
of mastery which progressively increases. There is, then, a clear
indication here of a move from interest and delight in sound towards
control of materials: the first important shift in the musical development of very young children.

Moog identifies another important change during the second
year, this time concerning movement to music. Somewhere between
the age of 18 months and 2 years, children begin to 'match their
movements to the rhythm of the music'. This is rather fitful and
short-lived and not every child does this, but it is surely the first
presage of response to expressive character in music. When a person
moves to music, what we see is a physical *imitation* of sonorous
gestures or character and, although spontaneous movement to music
tends to diminish in the later years of infancy, its presence at this
stage is a helpful outward manifestation of an early imitative
response.

One further example from the work of Moog serves to reinforce
this theoretical picture of musical engagement and supports the idea
that there is a sequence of musical development, if only we are
patient enough to look for it. Moog notes that a new category of
singing emerges at around the age of 4. He calls these utterances
'imaginative songs', and fortunately the word imaginative here coincides with the Piagetian definition of it (unlike his use of the word
'imitative' which refers only to being able to reproduce or copy a
song). Some of these imaginative songs tell stories, some of them are

59

totally novel and some incorporate elements of songs already known but reconstituted in new ways. Here then is a hint of the emergence of imaginative play, the forming of new structural relationships from scraps of tunes already absorbed during earlier stages, though Moog would not consider the 4-year-old capable of 'original creation' (p.21). By the time these children come to school they have musically visited every corner of the theoretical triangle, though the processes lag well behind language development, probably because most adults do not 'music' back to children as they 'language' back to them. Mastery is most evident but there are the first fitful glimmers of imitation and imaginative play. Development, though, does not stop here. Each mode of playfulness will be revisited and given a stronger emphasis at different times during childhood.

Children's compositions

The most direct and uncomplicated way of extending developmental studies into school age is to observe the musical compositions of children, just as studies of language development concentrate on what children actually say or write. I define 'compositions' very broadly and include the briefest utterances as well as more sustained invention. Composition takes place when there is some freedom to choose the ordering of music, with or without notational or other forms of detailed performance instruction. Others may prefer at times to use the terms improvisation, invention or 'creative music'. All of these fall within this very broad definition of 'composition', the act of assembling music.

June Tillman, working as a research student with me in the London University Institute of Education, spent many years collecting and analysing compositions, initially from children aged 3 to 11 years, though later from older children too (Swanwick and Tillman, 1986). She was teaching in South London schools in which there were children from many different ethnic and cultural groups, including some from Asian, West Indian, African, Northern and Southern European backgrounds. The children whose work she observed were, as far as possible, representative of this mix and included some having individual or group instrumental lessons and many who did not.

All of the children had class music lessons with the researcher/ teacher varying in length from 20 minutes a week for the 3- to 4-year-olds, two half-hours each week for the 5- to 7-year-olds and one half-hour a week for the 8- to 9-year-olds. In some classes, especially of younger children, these musical activities were followed up by the class teacher. The lessons all included opportunities for musical composition and performance and some of the older children were involved in quite long projects, including composing music for stories of some half-hour's duration, sometimes combining with dance and drama. There was then, a context of active musical involvement.

Each child was given opportunities to make music in a variety of ways. For the purposes of this research, the following possibilities were chosen as representing a range of the available instruments, arranged in a rough sequence of increasing complexity:

1. A pair of maracas;
2. A tambour played with the hand;
3. A choice of instruments with which s/he would be familiar (tambour, maraca, Indian cymbal, triangle, claves, castanets, tambourine), including the maracas and tambour already played;
4. A choice of instruments with which s/he was not familiar;
5. Chime bars of E, G and A with one beater;
6. A xylophone with a pentatonic scale and two beaters;
7. A metalophone organized with the scale of C major along with two beaters;
8. A fully chromatic xylophone with two beaters;
9. Asked to 'say something' like 'It is sunny and I am happy' on any of the instruments available;
10. Asked to make up a song, either with words, or humming or 'lahing'.

The children were given time to be satisfied with what they had composed and every child was asked to play each composition a second time in order for us to estimate the extent of musical memory and observe which elements of the composition survived repetition. All these musical utterances were recorded three times each term; 745 compositions from 48 children over four years, along with some additional pieces from older children. We were, then, looking not only at a cross-section of children at different ages, but in some cases, at the same children over a period of time, sometimes several years.

A first analysis

The first step was to take a small sample of this vast musical out-
put and to ask three independent judges to listen to an edited tape-
recording containing three items from each of seven children,
ranging from the age of 3 to 9. The age of each child was not
revealed and the presentation of age order was randomized. These
judges were asked to rank the ages of the children from the evidence
they heard on the tape. One of the judges, a teacher but not experienced musically, found this task almost impossible and said so, but
the others, who were both musicians and experienced teachers,
managed the task without too much difficulty and gave interesting
reasons why they thought that a particular group of compositions
were from an older or a younger child. These comments were
frequently to do with the level of technical control and musical
organization.

When we looked at the estimated ages given by the two appropriately experienced judges and compared them with the actual age
of the children, we found quite a strong statistical correlation.

Figure 2: Judges estimate the age of children by listening to their compositions

Actual ages	9	8	7	6	5	4	3
Judge 1	8	9	7	4	5	6	3
Judge 2	7	8	9	4	5	6	3

There did appear to be observable differences between the musical
compositions of these children, linked with age. We then felt fairly
secure in making our own judgements about the remaining pieces.
The questions were: what is the nature of these differences? Could
the compositions be grouped into a theoretical framework that
related in any way to the idea that music was a form of extended
play, having a triangle of elements? As these questions began to
be answered, it became possible to develop and refine a more
sophisticated model; not by pulling categories out of 'thin air', but
by attending carefully to what children had actually produced.

Towards a model of musical development

The emergent picture was strikingly confirmed by Malcolm Ross, who puts forward his own description of the process of aesthetic development in the arts. For the purposes of comparison with our own analysis, it will serve to paraphrase here some of the key statements made by Ross, outlining as he does four periods of development in music; developmental categories that coincide with his descriptions of what he regards as similar processes in art and drama (Ross, 1984: 129–30).

1. *Years 0–2*   Ross sees this as a time of pure sensuous engage-ment with sound materials, along with experimentation and the beginnings of relating music to feeling or mood.
2. *Years 3–7*   This stage is characterized by musical doodling, especially vocally, and by the progressive mastery of what Ross calls 'sound structures and patterns'. He notes the beginning of anticipa-tion in music. In art and drama he begins to see perception of expressive gesture developing, of signs as 'representative' of experience.
3. *Years 8–13*   This, for Ross, is marked by concern with the 'con-ventions of musical production', a desire to 'join the adult scene'. Programme or 'narrative and descriptive music makes sense'. There is a desire to become 'conventionally proficient' and teachers must 'satisfy the demand for greater conventional competence'. The important element here is that of working within an accepted musical idiom.
4. *Years 14 +*   Here music is seen as taking on greater significance as a form of personal expression, 'embodying, meaning and vision', significant for an individual or for a community.

I have argued (after Meyer), that musical structure depends on our having musical expectations. If we accept Ross's observation — that powers of anticipation begin to develop during the second stage — as signifying the beginnings of this awareness of structural rela-tionships, then the over-arching sequence of development seems to run through *mastery* and *imitation* to *imaginative play*. This is indeed what we were to find in our analysis of the children's compositions.

I would emphasize here a point to be elaborated later, that each one of these 'stages' or, perhaps better, *transformations*, is swept up into the succeeding developmental thrust. We do not merely pass through one of these modes but carry them forward with us into the next. At times it is necessary to begin again. For example, if we handle a new instrument, or work in a new idiom, or on a new piece of music, we are sent immediately back to the problems of mastery. It is important to be clear these transformations are both cumulative and cyclical.

We were further influenced by some observations of Robert Bunting which appeared as Working Paper 6 of the Schools Council Project, *Music in the Secondary School Curriculum* (1977). This short paper has as its focus the idea of the *vernacular*, 'the common language of music', what Ross calls the 'conventions of musical production'. Bunting identifies several modes of musical engagement and his descriptions relate well to our emergent development sequence, though he is not especially concerned to order these modes in a developmental way. From our analysis of over 700 compositions and from his categorisation we feel able to map out a series of processes which make up the following developmental sequence (Bunting, 1977).

Mastery: sensory response and manipulation

Bunting employs the terms neurological; acoustical; mechanical. The neurological mode he describes as 'the reaction of the nervous system of sensations of timbre, rhythm, pitch, quite independently of the analytical mind'. He notes that the use of very high or low pitches or loud or soft instrumentation brings the neurological impact of music to the fore. At one remove from this, the acoustical mode has to do with the interaction of sound with the size and design of the buildings in which music is played. We can be 'affected as much by the degree of resonance sound is given, as by its pitch or syntactical meaning'. He gives as instances the use of open strings and mutes or the use of space and distance for musical impact. In the compositions of our very young children at the age of 3 or 4, we observed a keen interest in very soft and very loud sounds; a loud bang on a drum accompanied by expressions of sheer delight or even fear, or a fascination with the very gentle sounds of a shaker or Indian cymbal. Both the neurological and the acoustical mode are evident in the young child's primary concern with the tone and resonance of instruments, experimenting with short and long sounds, slow and fast shakes, or fingers and fists on the surfaces of drums.

The 'mechanical' impulse can be seen at work when the physical aspects of instruments themselves determine the organization of the music; as when the alternation of two drumsticks or a pair of beaters produces trills or *tremolos* and leaping, angular melodies, or when children simply play up and down whatever scale series is set up on the instruments. This way of making up music, along with the enjoyment of repeating musical fragments, was frequently and obviously present in the compositions of our 4- to 5-year-olds. One consequence of the mastery impulse is that compositions tend to become repetitious, even to the point of appearing to ramble.

Imitation: personal expression and the vernacular

Bunting uses the term *illustrative*, which he defines as 'a way of giving music meaning by association'. This is one of the directly associative ways of respoding to music which were identified in the psychological literature in Chapter 2. As an example, Bunting instances the device of a drum-roll signifying thunder, noting that it can also lend itself to the more subtle possibility of signifying anger. This is an important difference. Within the category of *imitation*, we could include rather crude direct copying of sounds using musical instruments. It so happens that this making of 'sound effects' is rarely present in the musical work of children we studied, nor is it observed by Moog at younger ages. Even at its simplest and amongst the youngest, music is much more abstract than this. Anger can certainly be heard in a drum-roll.

As I argued earlier, there is a powerful tendency for music to be expressive, without being in any way illustrative, or representational. Music rarely appears to have a conveniently describable 'subject', yet does seem to contain an expressive charge: we hear gestures, character and movement in music through the processes of identifiable posture and gestural change. Bunting appears to believe that this level of musical experience, which he calls the 'symbolic mode', appears late, towards the end of schooling if at all. In this he may be misled by children's responses going 'underground', blocking out the gaze of the outside observer, especially in adolescence. We detect this abstract expressive quality much earlier on in the musical behaviour of children. Bunting puts it rather well and echoes Langer when he says that:

> musical rhythms and tensions seem to mirror the flow of feeling within us in a direct, non-verbal and non-illustrative way. Most of us would consider this music's most important quality and it is not a thinking process but a feeling one. (p.4)

It is in the songs of children that the first signs of imitation, acts of musical *expression*, begin to appear. It may be that the personal and relatively 'non-technical' nature of the human voice makes early expression more likely, and several instances of clear expressive characterization were noted in songs, even at the age of 4, though by the fifth year instrumental compositions also begin to be characterful. Deliberate changes in levels of speed and loudness along with the use of wider or closer intervals reveal an expressive intention which is not confined to illustration or sound effects.

This early flowering of musical expressiveness frequently bears little relationship to recognizable musical conventions and seems to derive directly from the pleasure of manipulating sound materials. One little girl of 4 produced a song in response to the idea of the sun shining which simply and powerfully caught up the word 'shine' into an exuberant expressive melody (Swanwick and Tillman, 1986). The sounds themselves, the physical feeling of singing, even the sensation of the word 'shine' in the mouth, appear to lead the way with little reference to any other songs she might know. And this is by no means a kind of picture, or illustration, of sunshine. In a clear act of imitation, of expressive characterization, she seemed to shine herself; but it is an inner glow, not that of a heavenly body; metaphorical and no more literal than when we say of someone that she has a 'sunny disposition'.

An important shift takes place during these early years when *imitation* seems to dominate the musical landscape; a move from the personal and idiosyncratic production of music still closely linked to sonorous impact and experiment, towards socially shared *vernacular* conventions. The imitative aspect of expressiveness may begin as *personal* expression but is soon swept up into a community of musical commonplaces; shaped phrases and received melodies, steady pulse and metric rhythm patterns, syncopations and repeated tonal formulas. What Bunting calls 'the common language of music' takes over as the dominant influence, as learned songs are incorporated into the musical inventions of children, as metrical patterns and phrase are absorbed from a broad musical culture. Moog noticed this to some extent in the singing of his 4-year-olds but it becomes much more evident in our subjects by around the age of 7, when musical gestures are more stylized, borrowed from tradition. Gardner, too, notes that by the age of 7 or so, children's work in the arts is characterized in part by becoming 'socialized', drawing on the cultural 'code' (Gardner, 1973): what Ross calls the 'conventions of musical production'.

This is not an expressiveness arising directly from the child's personal state of feeling but an entry into a shared world of musical ideas, where, sometimes, expressive character appears to be second-hand. This may seem even to be regressive, a loss of creativity and spontaneity but it is certainly important and necessary if children are to share musical procedures and enter a musical community. Their compositions at this time are not without characterization but the expressive gestures tend to be borrowed, as common rhythmic or melodic patterns are adopted, or when fairly conventional answering phrases appear — unambitious musical ideas. Frequently, melodies that are already known are reproduced, sometimes altered and sometimes used, perhaps, as subconscious models.

Of course, just as we shall still find examples of sensory exploration and manipulative interest, it is also possible, through the ages of about 5 to 8, to find direct personal expressiveness. The main thrust of development, though, is from the *personal* to the *vernacular*, from individual expressiveness to that which is socially shared. As Ross puts it: there is a desire to become 'conventionally proficient'. As I shall try to show in the next chapter, this desire returns again in a much stronger form at the third main transformation which is related to Piaget's concept of imaginative play.

Figure 3 is a sketch of the picture so far. It takes the form of a spiral for several reasons, one of which is that the process is cyclical; we never lose the need to respond to sound materials, re-entering the spiral repeatedly, no matter what age we happen to be or how musically experienced we are. Furthermore, the process is cumulative; when making music, sensory sensitivity and manipulative control interact with each other and, later on, with personal and conventional expressiveness.

A third reason for the spiral form of representation is the apparent recurring pendulum swing in musical development, from the individual and idiosyncratic perspective to the socially stimulating and communally responsive. At the lower level, that of *materials*, the *sensory* element is highly individualistic and exploratory whilst the *manipulative* is both prompted by and required for social sharing. We can explore the qualities of sound quite easily alone but if we want to play with others, then the manipulative ability to repeat, to control, to synchronize, to modify, and to balance becomes prime. Similarly, expressiveness can only be shared with others through a system of mutually held conventions.

Figure 3: The sequence of early musical development (Swanwick and Tillman, 1986)

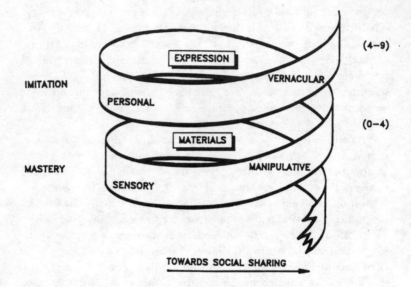

Daniel has now just passed his third birthday and is still asking to play the guitar whenever he comes to see us. One day,
I am in the bathroom and the other grown-ups are elsewhere.
We suddenly hear the CD player. He has selected the Bream
recording from the rack and has turned on the amplifier and
the disc unit, found the switch that opens the drawer, inserted
the disc and pressed 'play'.

We discover him sitting there, guitar across his middle,
listening to the music. I say that we could march on all-fours
to it and we do. Then the character of the piece changes but
he seems not to notice and carries on 'marching'. 'Let's do

something else', I say, 'and march again when the music marches.' The musical reprise is very obvious, its expressive character reverts to what it was before. He does not seem to notice. I am by now not surprised. He is a bright little boy, but a bit young, according to our research, to pay much attention to expressive character. His mind is still focused towards the sensory elements of music and he is just beginning to enjoy some small degree of mastery. Why should I worry him with the next turn of the spiral? In a while perhaps . . . ?

5

Musical development beyond infancy

Exactly in what manner we sort out and add up and realize
in our own minds the impressions that can only be gained
singly in the separate moments of the music's flowing past
us is surely one of the rarer manifestations of consciousness.
Here if anywhere the imagination must take fire.

(Aaron Copland, *Music and Imagination*: 25)

Comparatively few writers seem concerned to study human development beyond the early years. It is, admittedly, more difficult than
the study of very young children, since social and environmental
variables become more obviously powerful as we grow up and it
becomes very awkward to untangle maturation from education,
nature from culture, the genetic inheritance of people from the influence of their life situation. Of course, there is a literature on
'adolescence', a recognition that this is an identifiable phenomenon
in most if not all cultures. There are also the highly speculative and
influential theories of writers such as Erikson. He postulates eight
stages of psycho-social development, ending in later adulthood with
the polarity of 'integrity versus despair', with a possible positive
outcome of 'renunciation and wisdom' (Erikson, 1963).

If we are generally reluctant to classify the years beyond early
childhood as potential times of 'development', then this seems to
be an error. It is indeed easier to look at a child and watch the
positive changes; perhaps not so fascinating or naturally attractive
to try to observe the subtle and sometimes slower evolution of mind
and behaviour in adults. This ought not to deter us from trying
to understand what motivates and sustains people of any age. Every
observant teacher or parent knows that there is a broad pattern of
development throughout the years of schooling and every writer

of the calibre of Shakespeare knows that there are a number of 'ages of man', phases in life that are to some extent predictable, or at least very probable. Schumann's setting of the poems of Chamisso, *Frauenliebe und Leben*, written near the start of the nineteenth century with European woman in mind, strikes a chord of recognition in people of both sexes across the world. From a literary aspect at least, the work is an archetype of a lifetime sequence of loving and losing. Just as education is more than schooling, so human development is more than what happens in early childhood.

Some may be horrified at the very thought of a recognizable sequence of development, perhaps believing that it stems from a mechanistic or deterministic view of the universe and leads to stereotyping, a denial of human individuality. Not so. If we think of those people who at various times have been most helpful to us, we shall probably notice that they were not only sympathetic or kind, but also understanding, having some repertoire of expectations on which to draw. We were probably not the first to come to them with a particular kind of problem. People may sometimes be surprising but they are rarely totally unpredictable; there are fairly universal patterns of growth, recognizable sequences of mind and feeling and we understand ourselves and others better if we acknowledge them, working along with the currents and tides of nature.

In this chapter, I want to follow the idea of musical development beyond early childhood. I think that we can learn more about musical 'intuition' and music education in this way. So far, our observations of children, taken along with hints and nudges in the literature, suggest that the earliest mode of musical experience, the first thrust of development, consists in the transformation of pure sensory delight in sounds into an urge for mastery; an emphasis on the exploration and control of the materials of music. The second transformation is from personal expressiveness to expression within general vernacular conventions. I now want to consider a third mode of development, where the imaginative play impulses motivate speculative forays into musical structure, which eventually become transformed into stylistic or idiomatic understanding.

Imaginative play: speculation and the idiomatic

Bunting writes: 'a composer may seek out new ideas by speculating on accepted musical conventions. Extreme cases are atonality and indeterminacy but less radical speculations have always been part of our musical tradition' (Bunting, 1977). Musical speculation clearly depends on some fluency of manipulative ability *and* on an awareness of certain shared conventions of expressiveness. There has to be a context of socially recognized musical possibilities in order to create and respond to surprises. We are not able to deviate from norms unless we actually work from them. Around the age of 10, though usually closer to 11, we observed in children's compositions the emergence of *speculation* out of the commonplaces of the *vernacular*. It is on this ability to identify new relationships that any grasp of musical form is predicated. Making sense of the flow of music involves, as Copland says, the imagination taking fire.

First attempts by children to be musically speculative in their compositions sometimes appear to be a regression to earlier stages of manipulative insecurity. Some of the earlier fluency and confidence seem to be lost in this new phase of experimentation which, for the children we were observing, was often focused on melodic development. To give a couple of instances: a boy of 11 in one composition appeared to be speculating with tonal inversion, trying to turn his phrases upside down; a song by a girl of 11 embodied a bold attempt at atonality, though she had to search hard for the particular order of the notes she wanted within this framework of totally new relationships. Often there was a clear ending 'tag', a kind of 'punch line', not possible without a degree of security in the grasp of the vernacular.

The expectations aroused by a familiar and repeated pattern give rise to surprise if they are not gratified in some predictable way. This is why the dreadful limerick by W.S. Gilbert has at least some minimal effect: it begins something like; 'There was a young man of Trallee/Who was horribly stung by a wasp'. One of the first signs of structural exploration, of imaginative play, is found in this kind of changed ending after a fairly ordinary start; to be found in many jokes, and, as we saw earlier, in poetry too. At this level of musical encounter, there is a still a tremendous attraction in handling sound materials with musical expressiveness: but the *speculative* mode initiates a new concern for musical form, for making music which is not only characterful but also coherent.

The speculative impulse can still be seen at work within sometimes strongly derivative idiomatic compositions — the next transformation. At this stage, compositions may be modelled closely on the style of admired musicians or even on one particular piece.

An example of this process occurs in a piece by pupils of Brian Loane, to be heard on the tape accompanying the *British Journal of Music Education* (Vol. 1, No. 3). A piece called 'Escape' by a group of 11- to 12-year-olds bears more than an accidental resemblance to a song by the pop group 'Madness': 'Night Boat to Cairo'. This is not just a simple 'copy' but is given a novel speculative edge, partly by taking up implications of words to do with a desert island, 'the island where we are free'.

Frequently in the early teens, the chosen idiom falls within the range of rock and pop music, though it is possible to find strong commitments to other styles among young people between the ages of 10 and 15. Stylistic authenticity is at a premium and is frequently linked with dress, social behaviour — complete life-style. These issues wait to be discussed in a subsequent chapter but for the moment, it is enough to say that teachers of music and parents of young people at around this age commonly report resistance to anything but the accepted idiom. In some instances it may even seem that imaginative or speculative activity goes underground, giving way to cliché.

Speculation is still alive though and often emerges as inventiveness within the adopted set of musical conventions. We were able to study some work of people above the age of 11 or 12 and noted several compositions from the 14- to 15-year-old age-group which demonstrated very well-assimilated idioms. For example, one small group of girls produced a composition which started from the programmatic idea of 'Storm', organized around a clearly idiomatic motif in a 'laid-back' swing idiom. Towards the middle of the composition came the 'storm' passage based on note clusters, an idea adapted from a contemporary piece recently heard at a concert. This eventually gives way to a reprise of material associated with the first motif. Musical features from two quite different traditions are thus deliberately juxtaposed in an act of musical speculation across two idioms. Work for the GCSE examination is beginning to bring forward much more evidence of speculation being carried forward into idiomatic practices.

Meta-cognition: symbolic valuing and systematic engagement

I would project a fourth level of development which may occur after the age of about 15 years and subsumes the earlier manifestations of mastery, imitation and imaginative play. The new emphasis is on what psychologists call *meta-cognition*. Techically, meta-cognition is the term used to label the process of becoming aware of and articulating ideas about our own thought processes. I am using the term here in a slightly more limited and special sense: indicating self-awareness of the processes of thought and feeling in a value-response to music. Central to this awareness is the development of a steady and often intense commitment to what Bunting calls 'the inner emotional content of music at a personal level'. A strong sense of *value*, often publicly declared, permeates this mode of musical experience. Music has meaning for an individual at a high level of personal significance.

This transformation coincides with other developments frequently noted in the mid-teens: fervent religious commitment; zealous political affiliation; intense personal relationships and ardent hero-worship. We may ourselves have experienced them. People are not only intensely self-aware at this time but may also need to reflect on, perhaps to talk with others about their experiences, feelings and emerging value perspectives. From a cognitive psychological perspective, Jerome Bruner, in *Towards a Theory of Instruction* puts it this way:

> intellectual growth involves an increasing capacity to say to oneself and others, by means of words or symbols, what one has done or what one will do. This self-accounting or self-consciousness permits the transition from merely orderly behaviour to logical behaviour, so called. It is the process that leads to the eventual recognition of logical necessity — the so-called analytic mode of the philosophers — and takes human beings beyond empirical adaptation.
>
> (Bruner, 1966: 15)

Although the transition from the *idiomatic* mode into this new level of awareness is gradual, sometimes imperceptible, there is a qualitative difference between socially stimulated commitment to a particular musical idiom and the first stage of what I am calling meta-cognitive development: in musical terms, the *symbolic*. The main shift can be seen in the tendency for individuals to find that music of a particular kind, or even one particular piece, begins to correspond with special frames of mind. They may have what amounts to a 'love affair' with a composition, even a chord sequence. One line of poetry in a song may assume tremendous significance. Musical and other preferences are not now determined primarily by social consensus, by a 'teeny-bopper' craze or fad. It is possible to see in this new level of commitment the first full flowering of musical valuing, involving all the previous levels of response infused with a strong element of self-actualization; at a time when people can be overwhelmed by the intensity of their feelings, becoming acutely conscious of the fast-expounding boundaries of self.

It may be for some, that such a level of response to music is never or rarely reached. Whether or not this need be so is another question, but I cannot escape the conclusion that not to be able to so respond is a form of under-development. Of course it is true that everyone is potentially musical, in the same way that everyone is, to coin a word, 'languageal': but this is not to say that musical development can survive lack of stimulation and nurturing, any more than language acquisition can. There have been cases of children deprived of linguistic and social interaction, such as Peter the 'wolf' boy who, through odd circumstances, missed out on childhood in human society. Following this deprivation he was never able ever to converse at a later age. There is such a thing as musical deprivation too. Ultimately, we can only value what we know and understand and this will depend on the richness of the musical environment and our cumulative interaction with the elements of music.

The ultimate development within the meta-cognitive, or value mode, might most appropriately be called the *systematic*. The evidence for this lies in the writings of musicians, especially composers, where a strong sense of personal value leads to the development of systematic engagement. New musical universes may be mapped out, and this creation of musical systems can be observed either in new generative musical procedures — we could think of Schoenberg and serial technique — or of talking and writing about music in a way that might be musicological, aesthetic, historical, scientific, psychological or philosophical. Instances of musicians in the west who have reflected systematically on the nature of music and its value would include Hindemith, Tippett, Cage and Copland. India, China and the Arab world also have an analytical and philosophical literature of this kind. Not only is the value of music strongly felt and publicly declared, but the field is subjected to detailed critical analysis and development; musical potential is expanded by new processes or perspectives.

Figure 4 shows the full developmental spiral. The age indications

Figure 4: The spiral of musical development (Swanwick and Tillman, 1986)

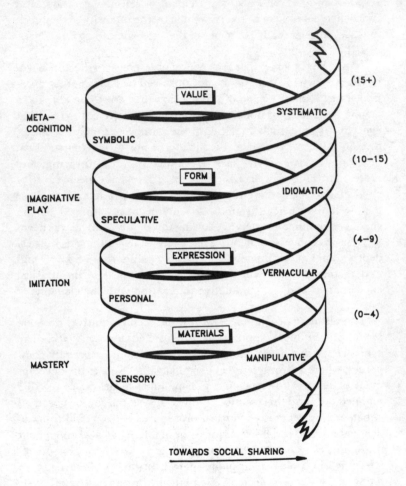

in brackets refer only to the children whose compositions we have studied, though, as I have indicated, there is some support in the literature for a more general interpretation of the sequence.

Eight developmental modes

It might be helpful here to identify the main characteristics of the developmental modes I have been trying to describe.

Sensory

Up to about the age of 3, young children are directly responsive to the impressiveness of sound, particularly timbre. There is a fascination with dynamic levels, especially with extremes of loud and soft. There is much 'strumming' — experimentation with instruments and other sound sources. At this level, the elements of music are pretty disorganized; pulse is unsteady and variations of tone colour appear to be musically arbitrary, having no apparent structural or expressive significance. Unpredictable and fitful sound exploration is characteristic of these early years.

Manipulative

Children are acquiring a steadier interest in the techniques involved in handling instruments. They begin to organize regular pulse and start to use technical devices suggested by the physical structure and layout of available instruments; such as *glissandi*, scalic and intervallic patterns, trills and *tremolo*. Compositions tend to be long and rambling as children enjoy the repetitions of a mastered device, before moving on in an arbitrary way to the next possibility. Increasing control in the manipulative mode is most apparent in the compositions of children around the age of 4 and 5.

Personal expressiveness

Direct personal expression appears firstly and most evidently in song. During singing and instrumental pieces, expressiveness becomes apparent in the exploitation of changes of speed and loudness levels, often deliberately getting faster and louder in a fairly shapeless way. There are signs of elementary phrases — musical gestures — which are not always able to be repeated. There is little structural control and the impression is of spontaneous and unco-ordinated musical ideas emanating directly from the immediate feel-ings of children without critical reflection and shaping; 4 to 6 years seems to be the optimum time for personal expressiveness.

The vernacular

Patterns begin to appear — melodic and rhythmic figures that are able to be repeated. Pieces are often quite short, compared with those in the mode of personal expressiveness, and they are contained within established fairly general musical conventions. In particular, melodic phrases begin to fall into standard 2, 4 or 8-bar units. Metrical organization is common, along with such common devices as syncopation and melodic and rhythmic *ostinati* and sequences. Children have entered the first phase of conventional music-making. Their compositions are often very predictable and show that they have absorbed musical ideas from elsewhere while singing, play-ing and listening to others. Sometimes existing melodies are pro-duced as though they were the child's own creation. As Gardner says, the work of children at this age is often 'prosaic and drab', compared with the idiosyncratic earlier years (Gardner, 1983: 311). The *vernacular* mode begins to appear at around the age of 5 but is more clearly established at 7 or 8.

The speculative

With the *vernacular* firmly engaged, the deliberate repetition of pat-terns makes way for imaginative deviation: the *speculative*. Surprises occur, though perhaps not fully integrated into the style of a piece. Control of pulse and phrase — apparent at the earlier level — now appears less certain as children hunt for the 'right' note, or attempt a deviation that does not quite work. There is considerable experimentation, a desire to explore structural possibilities, looking to contrast or vary established musical ideas. One of the first ways of creating musical surprise, or speculation, is to have a novel ending after establishing musical norms by frequent repetition. Speculative compositions can sometimes be found earlier on, but the ages of 9 to

11 were the most common among the children we studied.

The idiomatic

Structural surprises now become more firmly integrated into a recognizable style. Contrast and variation take place on the basis of emulated models and clear idiomatic practices, frequently, though not always drawn from popular musical traditions. Young people of around 13 to 14 are particularly motivated to enter recognizable musical and social communities. Harmonic and instrumental authenticity is important for them. Answering phrases, call and response, variation by elaboration and contrasting sections are common, though sometimes the speculative element appears swamped by the need to conform to external models. Technical, expressive and structural control is established more reliably in longer compositions. The aim seems to be to move towards 'grown up' music-making by the emulation of accepted public performers, sometimes by composing pieces that strongly resemble existing influential models.

The symbolic

Growing out of the *idiomatic* is a strong personal identification with particular pieces of music. Particular musicians and pieces, even certain turns of phrase and harmonic progression can become highly significant for any individual. At the *symbolic* level there is a growing consciousness of music's affective power, coupled with a tendency to reflect on the experience and to articulate something of these responses to others. Commitment to music is founded on an intensity of personal feeling that is felt as significantly unique. The *symbolic* mode of musical experience is distinguished by the capacity to reflect upon musical experience and relate it to growing self-awareness and rapidly evolving general value systems. It seems unlikely that these meta-cognitive musical processes will be found before the age of about 15 and it is possible that some people rarely, perhaps never, experience this elevated mode of musical response.

The systematic

At the *systematic* level we might think of the highly developed person able to reflect on and be discursive about his or her musical experience in an intellectually organized way. There may be conscious exposition of the qualities underlying musical experience and an ability to make conceptual maps, which may be historical, musicological, psychological or philosophical. Musical composition at this level may be informed by research and the study and development of new systems, novel organizing principles. In the true sense of the term, we have an element of musical theorizing. Works may be based on sets of newly generated musical materials, such as a whole-tone scale, a note-row, a novel system of harmonic generation, electronically created sounds or computer technology. Aside from composing, people also talk and write about music as though it mattered; as critics, as researchers, as speculative thinkers. In the systematic mode, the universe of musical discourse is expanded, reflected upon, discussed and celebrated with others.

Figure 5: Children's compositions placed by developmental level

	Age									
	3	4	5	6	7	8	9	10	11	
Speculative	0	0	0	0	4	5	22	31	68	
Vernacular	0	2	1	12	21	39	29	18	64	
Personal	0	48	40	24	9	1	4	6	6	
Manipulative	18	129	19	14	12	8	3	0	4	
Sensory	31	45	3	0	4	1	0	0	0	
Total	49	224	63	50	50	54	58	55	142	745

Figure 5 shows the levels in the spiral which we judged were reached in 745 compositions across the age-range 3–11 years. It is important to remember that it is compositions that are being judged, not particular children; also that judgements attempt to determine only the presence of the highest observable level, assuming the inclusion of lower modes. For example, at the age of 7, there were 4 compositions judged to contain clear elements of speculation and 21 showing signs of control of vernacular techniques without any signs of speculation. 4 compositions were felt to be only at the sensory level and 12 were assigned to the manipulative category. No compositions reached the level of the convincingly idiomatic within the sample of this age-group. (Statistical probability based on a chi-square value of 1755.3 is $p < 0.001$.) Although there is a central tendency, at any age there is quite a wide spread of musical achievement.

All the indications are, then, that we can observe musical development and that it takes place in a certain sequence — the 'softer' meaning of the term development: certain developments may be necessary for later stages to occur. Our evidence, along with that of other researchers, suggests that there are sequential changes, though whether this is to what Maccoby calls a 'fairly standard timetable' is still undemonstrated, even if supported by other writers. With the children we observed there does indeed appear to be an unfolding pattern. I suspect that if children are in an environment where there are musical encounters, then this sequence will be activated. If the environment is particularly rich, then the sequence may be followed more quickly. The opposite may also, unfortunately, be true: in an impoverished musical environment, development is likely to be minimal, arrested.

Musical development and musical encounter

The process of musical development can be seen also as a map of the elements of musical response. The following brief description by a 17-year-old is of his first experience at a sitar recital. For twenty-five minutes he was not aware of any subtlety but wondered what was supposed to be happening. He goes on:

> What did happen was magic! After some time, insidiously the music began to reach me. Little by little, my mind — all my senses it seemed — were becoming transfixed. Once held by the soft but powerful sounds, I was irresistibly drawn into a new world of musical shapes and colours. It almost felt as if the musicians were playing *me* rather than their instruments, and so I, too, was clapping and gasping with every one else . . . I was unaware of time, unaware of anything other than the music. Then it was over. But it was, I am sure, the beginning of a profound admiration that I shall always have for an art form that has been, until recently, totally alien to me.
>
> (Dunmore, 1983: 20)

The writer here moves from being impressed by materials, 'soft and powerful sounds', to the expressive realm which he describes in the metaphor of 'shapes and colours', then towards structural appreciation, 'clapping and gasping', which suggests elements of formally generated surprise. Clearly, this young person writing about a single experience with Indian music has moved through the developmental transformations of the spiral to the level of being able to declare some value commitment. Indeed, in the act of describing the whole process of response for us, he shows that he tends towards the symbolic organization of his experience, analysing and sharing his findings.

This brings us to the issue of whether a model of musical development based on observation of children's composition can be addressed to the roles of the performer and being in audience to music. Any performance is clearly not going to be musically adequate unless it meets certain standards in at least the first six modes. The situation of the person in audience rests on the concept of *responsiveness*. The extent to which a person is able to respond to music depends significantly on the range of developmental modes that are open to him or her. What are people listening for? It is a great limitation to be aware *only* of the sonorous surface of music; a point made ironically, I think by Beecham, who said that the British dislike music but adore the sound it makes. Nor is it enough to admire only the manipulative fluency of performers: I am reminded of the wife of a headteacher in whose school I taught, who told me that she recognized instantly the musicality of one of the pupils because he had 'played the organ *faster* than anyone else'. Even recognition of expressive character is insufficient to help us find music cohesive or interesting — we soon lose the thread and fall back on day-dreaming, as Shaw describes (see Chapter 2). Ultimately, music educators are keen that people come to value music and this valuing is built, as it must be, on the activity of mind across all the other levels.

I ought to emphasize again that the developmental spiral has to be re-activated each time music is encountered, and certainly when we are faced with a new piece as performer or in audience or when composing/improvising. The first and most striking impression of music is always its sensory surface, especially if we have been deprived of music for any length of time. Unlike very young children though, more experienced people can move on to engage with the other elements which add new layers of significance to responsiveness.

The ability to interpret sensitively and encourage the musical engagement of individuals is crucial to effective teaching. The modes of the spiral not only are developmental descriptions but also can be seen as layers in the language of musical engagement and therefore of musical *criticism*. I would go so far as to say that any observations a music critic might make are bound to fall within one or other of these modes. Far from stereotyping our expectations of what students at any age might musically achieve, an understanding of what music really *is* may go some way to increase the richness of our responses. Essentially, the teacher of music is a music critic, in the best sense of that term, and needs to acquire a critical vocabulary.

The evolving theory

It now seems possible to propose that we have a theory of music and musical development which gathers together some of the scattered elements of research in psychology and integrates them into a comprehensive view of music. In the first chapter, I tried to draw out certain 'philosophies' of music education. One of these emphasized individual creativity: in other words, concentrated its focus on the left-hand side of the spiral. Sensory delight, exploring sound, personal expression and speculative imaginative power are all, so to speak, on the left. The 'traditionalist' theory emphasizes the right-hand side: stressing manipulative or technical ability, a grasp of the vernacular conventions of music-making and idiomatic or stylistic authenticity. A curriculum perspective which picks out the idea of music relevance through Afro-American styles simply changes the idiomatic stance, relating musical tradition more strongly to local community values and contemporary society.

There are many fascinating questions to do with the pendulum swing from left to right, which is echoed historically in the 'romantic' versus 'classical' polarity. There are also as yet unanswered psychological questions waiting to be addressed, especially that of the relationship of accommodation and assimilation within the model. One thing though is certain: to try to actualize an educational philosophy without regard to the interaction of left and right would be like trying to clap with one hand. Bruner writes that myths, art, ritual and the sciences are all 'expressions of this deep-lying tendency to explicate and condense, to seek steady meaning in capricious experience' (1974: 31). It may be that the relationship between left and right is a sign of this deep dialectic process.

In the second chapter, I noted that the areas of research into the psychology of music had, in an haphazard manner, uncovered certain layers of music response. Earlier workers had settled for their own patch, whether of trying to measure the direct effects of sound; the associational 'meaning' processes, structural expectations or the preference patterns of musical valuing. The developmental spiral begins to map the musical relationships of these disparate pieces of work, seeing them as interactive and sequential, rather than as isolated areas of research.

Musical development and music education

There seem to be three general levels at which we can begin to see the implications of this developmental theory for musical transactions in classrooms and studios. I shall raise these here and try to spell out other consequences later on in the book. The first implication is in terms of broad curriculum planning, especially in schools. Our research at the Institute of Education into curriculum practice suggests that music education in schools seems somewhat arbitrary and that expectations of children at different ages are by no means clearly formed. The result of this is that it is not often possible to find progression over the period of compulsory education. Indeed, it might be said that the lack of a sense of progressive achievement may account for the disenchantment of pupils towards music in schools; a negative view that has been observed more than once, especially by the middle years of British secondary schooling (Francis, 1987).

If this assessment is anywhere near correct, then one overall curriculum implication of the theoretical model under discussion is that we might focus curriculum activities towards specific aspects of musical development at different broadly identified stages. At least we might try consciously working with the grain of children's development, something that those rare and intuitively gifted teachers do almost by instinct.

In the very early years of schooling and at pre-school level, sensory exploration and the encouragement of limited manipulative control would be the main aim. In the primary school this could be taken further forward and the imitative elements of music would come more sharply into focus, perhaps at times as the centre of our work: grounded in personal expression and exploration of sound but moving also towards the acquisition of vernacular skills. This work could be integrated with movement and dance and related to visual images which help to promote, stimulate and intensify expressiveness. By the age of 10 or so we would be looking to further the production and recognition of musical speculation, for an understanding that all musical form depends on contrasts and repetitions and that surprises are crucial to musical structure.

This development may be transformed through adolescence into an idiomatic 'hardening of the arteries'. Even so, the speculative can be kept alive while young people enter a 'grown-up' world (rather than the classroom world) of music. Much re-organization of resources will be needed in order to convert present opportunities into something that more nearly matches the development of children and the demands of music; including appropriate instruments and other equipment along with the expertise of different teachers, so that there can be some basis of choice for the student who is becoming idiomatically aware.

The second way in which such a model may inform the music curriculum concerns individual development. It ought to be possible for a teacher to identify where a child is on the spiral at any time. Although we may teach classes, people develop as individuals. If we are aware of the next likely mode of development for example, that pleasure in manipulative ability may lead to personal expression or that engagement in the vernacular may move into the more imaginatively speculative then we are more likely to ask the right kind of question, to suggest a more relevant possibility, to choose material or suggest an activity that may have more personal meaning and consequence for the individual.

This has just as much significance for the studio teacher as for the teacher in school classrooms. As we saw in the third chapter, the setting up of sets of sound material to be controlled at different technical levels — chord patterns, scale formations, jazz riffs and so on — can be very helpful, not only to the composer, but also to the instrumentalist or singer. To take just one aspect of this: it is essential not to lose touch with the sensory element in pursuit of technical fluency. In a conversation I had with Hans Keller, he complained that scales and exercises had ruined many music students; they manipulated the instrument without listening, without delight in the sound or expressive purpose. Each student has different needs at certain times: these might be more clearly identified by reference to the elements of the developmental spiral and we can keep reminding ourselves of what music is all about.

A third set of implications for the music curriculum has to do with the creative role of the teacher. How, for example, do we propose to start up an activity, to introduce a new musical procedure

or idea? For instance, take a fairly simple example of a compositional project. We may have decided to base this activity on the
fairly basic materials of short and long sounds. Let us make sure
that the first stage of the *sensory* is properly entered, that sounds
are savoured, no matter what the age or previous experience of the
students. There are different degrees of shortness and a very long
sound has a very different sensory effect from one that is only
moderately long. These perceptions are an important pre-condition
for sensitive *manipulative* control. Now we must learn how to sustain long sounds, what techniques may be involved on different
instruments, the use of beaters or bows, for example, to continually
activate sound as a tremolo. We might now move to explore the
expressiveness potential of combining short and long sounds into
mood or gesture. Is each student able to generate musical character,
whether dramatic or atmospheric, from short and long sounds? Is
this expressive quality communicated to others? We might then consider how these sounds can be caught up and found in existing
musical practices, the *vernacular*. Are they organized within a
framework or pulse and metre or do they draw on other musical
conventions? If the children are above the age of about 9, we shall
certainly want to edge them towards the *speculative*. Can they create
a surprise using short and long sounds? Can they make a piece that
holds the interest? Can we devise episodes or passages that relate
to one another as contrasts or repetitions? Are we concerned to
broaden the range of what is considered to be acceptable in *idiomatic*
terms? This will certainly lead us to encounter the music of others,
as performers or in audience.

It might be that a clear grasp of the concepts that I have attempted to articulate here may help us to understand a little more of
what is *musical* about music, in whatever branch of music and music
education we happen to be engaged. For example, once we grasp
that musical expression is a form of imitation then we can immediately see relationships with movement, drama, poetry, and visual
images; we can also understand how music can be expressive
without necessarily representing anything else, that a musical
gesture is an abstraction of physical gestures. We may use programmatic ideas to get the imitative process going but will always avoid
the literal translation of objects or events into music and will be
alert to the next thrust of development — musical speculation.

What is being suggested here is an attitude towards music curriculum development. We can start from exploration of a set of
musical materials, then, no matter how tightly or loosely we organize

the learning process, we shall be looking for the next question to ask. Asking the next question depends on having an idea as to what possible developments might be 'round the corner'. In the spiral, so to speak, we have many corners. The transition from one mode to the next is often so smooth as to be almost unnoticed, though occasionally it will seem to occur as a leap. It is also possible and at times necessary to retrace our steps; moving back down the spiral in order to move forward more freely, drawing back to leap.

An awareness of these developmental possibilities must surely be helpful and we shall at least avoid the danger of predicating a curriculum upon a narrow view of musical response. We would certainly not wish to limit ourselves to one side of the spiral — to the sensory, to personal expressiveness and to the speculative, but will also notice the importance of manipulative skills, of entering the shared discourse of a general musical vernacular and participating in idiomatic procedures. If we observe what children actually *do* as musicians, we shall notice that crossing from side to side of the spiral seems to be a developmental necessity: it must therefore be an educational imperative.

Interlude: from theory to practice

At the beginning of this book, I attempted to respond to the professional necessity of establishing a rationale for music education, a theory in the positive sense of that word, based on an understanding of what music really is. Essentially, when we engage with and respond to music, we are extending our ways of making and taking the world through symbolic discourse: drawing on the deep psychological wells of a universal play impulse in the exploration and communication of insights into the human condition. Music and the other arts share these fundamental processes of mind with other symbolic forms, such as science and philosophy.

The unique qualities of the arts lie not in the cultivation of special mental functions or states of feeling but in the intensity of their sensory impression, their expressive vividness of metaphor and imagery, in the coherence and concentration of their structural presentation. Their distinctive special symbolic mission lies in consciously celebrating living. Their ultimate value is that shared with all symbolic forms: they expand our universe of thought and feeling; they 'take us out of ourselves'. This they do most powerfully, frequently working simultaneously on several levels, contrapuntally. No cohesive community can get by without them.

From this perspective and through careful observation of children making music, it is possible to make a developmental 'map' which would give direction in teaching and curriculum planning. Research, particularly research with a psychological bias, would also gain from a theoretical overview of musical experience. I should re-emphasize the recurring cyclical and experiential nature of the developmental spiral: each new encounter with music reactivates on a smaller scale the process of the larger developmental sequence. This process was exemplified above through a description of musical encounter at a sitar recital (p. 81). Here then, very briefly, is a theory of music, the essential elements of musical development and experience.

The materials of music — sounds themselves — impress us with their sensory surface. Attention then focuses on how the sounds are made, on manipulative control, involving either directly or vicariously the pleasure of handling instruments, enjoying mastery, what Piaget calls 'virtuosity'. This opens out into a second transformation where the psychological processes of imitation lead us away from attending only to manipulative control towards the perception and production of expressive quality. This preoccupation with expressiveness may be at first very personal and idiosyncratic, perhaps shot through with extra-musical associations, giving way to concern with forms of expression that are more stylized, an interest in the commonplaces of the musical vernacular.

A subsequent transformation takes us to the realm of imaginative play, a psychological concept having its musical correlation in the ways we respond to and create formal relationships, bringing to music fluid sets of expectancies; speculating, predicting a future for ongoing music against a background of musical norms. These structural speculations eventually come to be located within clearly defined idioms, stylistic frames of reference which determine the kind of musical events that might reasonably be expected to happen. This leads on into a fourth level of transformation, building on idiomatic preferences, where music is consciously given a place in an evolving value system. A strong sense of the symbolic importance of music often permeates other commitments; for example, to religion or politics, or a philosophical world view, or to intense personal relationships or forms of hero-worship. For some, the symbolic significance of music may subsequently be carried forward into the systematic development of major new musical techniques, or may take the form of illuminating analysis or criticism, research, or other forms of sustained reflection upon musical experience.

In context and practice, music education consists in working out these elements in a context of institutional social, cultural and political values. The particular reality (not the only reality) of teaching, especially teaching in schools, may seem not to correspond too closely with what might be seen as an 'idealistic' view of music. Might we not have to settle for something less than the account of musical experience I have been trying to give? Are there not other ways of using music apart from the 'musical'? The answer to the second question is yes: music can be used for other than musical purposes. The answer to the first question has to be no: if we are in any way committed to music education, then facilitation of the richest possible musical experiences is our aim. In any case, my theory of music has strong roots in the work of others and has been fashioned from reflection on considerable direct musical experience, fused with careful observation of what children and other people actually *do* with music, in school and out. To this extent, the theory is grounded in practice.

Throughout the rest of this book I intend to put the theoretical basis to work in order to interpret and respond to three areas of practical difficulty and decision-making in music education: the cultural context; the making of a music curriculum and its evaluation; and the assessment of the musical work of students.

6

The cultural exclusiveness of music

All that counted was sound and the murderous mood it made.
All din and mad atmosphere. Really it was nothing but beat,
smashed and crunched and hammered home like some amaz-
ing stampede. The words were lost and the song was lost.

(N. Cohn, cited by B. Martin, *A sociology of
contemporary cultural change:* 160)

Valuing and labelling

As the quotation at the head of this chapter suggests, under certain
conditions musical response is certainly not as I have described it;
the 'song' can be lost in non-musical ends. Within the various
cultures that make up our society and inside the sub-cultures of
schools and colleges, there are other than musical issues to be
negotiated. Music education is only one strand of experience in a
web of social activities and community values. It is on this, the
fourth element of the map of musical experience that I now focus;
on the concept of *valuing*, trying to understand how and under what
conditions music may be valued and, more precisely, to what extent
any response to music may be caught up in and impeded by cultural
labelling, prejudice and stereotyping. (The more positive aspects
of the plurality of cultural contexts are considered in the following
chapter.)

It is undeniable that our perception of and response to music
is influenced by the position it is seen to occupy in a value
framework. This influence is probably much stronger than we often
suppose. As I shall show, systematic research and everyday observation suggest that people are not only predisposed to value

certain kinds of music for other than musical reasons, but they are likely to perceive the expressive and structural elements of music itself rather differently, depending on the attached value label.

For example, the musical value-worlds of regular listeners to Radio 3 and Radio 1 will tend to be sharply isolated from each other and within these general areas of musical preference there will be further subdivisions of preference and dislike. While the preferences of each individual evolve and fluctuate, there are usually clearly recognizable value clusters; combinations of what we read, how we choose to dress and do our hair, what form of speech we use, attitudes to others, and so on.

Within the field of popular music alone, we shall find distinctive elements of lifestyle across various groups of people whose musical worlds may be centred, say, around Reggae, Funk, Disco, Soul or Heavy Metal. At times, these lifestyles and the music that accompanies them go so closely together that the transmission of contradictory signals is felt as dissonant. For example, recently with a young relative I came across a teenager playing a tape of Led Zeppelin. The music was on for less than half a minute or so, but after the visitor had gone my companion observed that he had been listening to the 'wrong' music. He was not *dressed* appropriately, turned out as he was in a large black coat and topped with blond, possibly dyed hair. He should, I was told, be listening to New Wave or Soul or Funk but certainly not Heavy Metal. If he was really into Heavy Metal he should have been wearing a leather jacket, sport a pair of dirty jeans and have long greasy hair. The verdict was quite clear: 'he doesn't know his music'. His musical preferences and other cultural signals were discordant; the image was out of line. Perhaps such apparent contradictions are a sign of change, when a value-system is on the move, evolving, crumbling? In any event, unlike my relative, I would regard this breaking of a stereotype as a healthy act of cultural vandalism. Popular music, rock, opera and jazz are notorious for attracting strong peer-group affiliations, though we should be clear that the processes of labelling music and placing it within a social 'approval' context is universal and can be found just as easily within any category of the western classical or any 'folk' traditions.

Some of this fusion of music with general culture and lifestyle relies on obvious cultural mores which could be religious, political or fall into the general category of 'custom and practice'. Quite a lot of this cultural bonding relies on the adhesive of persuasion, the glue of propaganda, the attachment of labels. In an informal 'experiment', repeated several times, I asked groups of 30 to 40 students with newly acquired music degrees to listen to a short passage from a recording of Brahms' *First Symphony*. I then read a 'review' of this performance, followed by a critique of an alternative recorded version. This second record was then played — exactly the same passage. The musicians were then asked if they agreed with these reviews and an open discussion took place. Some rejected what was said by the 'critics' and a few suspicious people even went so far as to suggest that the reviews had been deliberately wrongly matched to the performances. Others more or less agreed with the critics. No one ever said, during any of these discussions, that they had listened to the same recording twice, though this was in fact the case. A little pantomime had taken place during which the record was replaced in its cover and, by sleight of hand, was taken out again and played on the same equipment, in the same room, at the same level of loudness; all this within five or ten minutes of the first playing.

What is particularly interesting is that many of the comments about the performance were critically quite well-developed, sensitively referring to subtleties of different phrasing, ensemble and speed. Yet, these perceptions could only be said to have resulted from the *value framework* within which the session was conducted; namely that a group of music graduates would be expected to find small and significant differences between performances if alerted by a lecturer to look for such differences by authoritative comments from alleged music 'critics'.

Such responses are similar in kind to those observed during the classic experiments of Asch (1951/1958), when subjects were asked to compare the relative length of lines. The social pressure to conform to the judgements of others was manipulated by a pre-arrangement — having everyone, or nearly everyone else in the group, agree to a particular though wrong consensus view. The level of compliance with the general view was in the order of 32 per cent if no confederate disagreed with the others, in spite of the fact that it seems very obvious their collective judgement was incorrect. Left to the socially uninfluenced judgement of their own eyes, people would not for a moment doubt where the truth really lay. After seeing A in Figure 6, subjects were asked to pick the matching line from B.

Figure 6: Which lines are the same length? (after Asch, 1951/58)

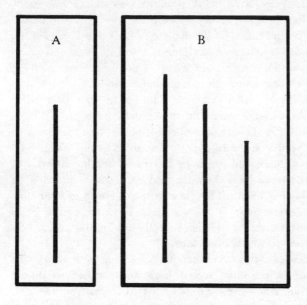

Davies, citing a procedure used by Weick *et al.*, notes that similar prestige effects are quite powerful among practising musicians (Davies, 1978). Two jazz orchestras were presented with three compositions, one of which was described as a 'serious' jazz work, another as a 'commercial', and therefore not so 'serious' a composition, while a third piece was unlabelled. The two orchestras heard the pieces in reverse order. Two main effects were noted. There were more playing errors in the performance of the piece regarded as 'not so serious' and, subsequently, recall of the so-called 'serious' composition was better than memory of the other. There are many difficulties about accepting the evidence from these experiments but it does seem likely that musicians might take a different attitude and play rather differently depending on whether or not the piece of music in hand was regarded by them as having high status rather than low. The labels we attach to music do seem to filter and shape the attitudes through which it is perceived and received.

Perhaps one of the most relevant and striking pieces of work in this area is that by Chapman and Williams (1976). Working with thirty-six 14- to 15-year-olds who were all self-declared 'progressive' thirty-six 14- to 15-year-olds who were all self-declared 'progressive pop' enthusiasts, they assigned them to three experimental groups on a random basis and eventually played to each group a two-minute extract of music composed by Takemitsu, *The Dorian Horizon*. One of the groups was used as an experimental 'control'. A second group was played two pieces of progressive pop music prior to hearing the Takemitsu work, a procedure intended to establish a particular frame of reference, a label category. This group then listened to *The Dorian Horizon* and were told that it was from an LP by a member of Pink Floyd, 'one of the best, if not *the* best, progressive band in the country at the moment'. The third group was played short extracts of 'classical' music by Bach and Beethoven prior to listening to the work by Takemitsu and were given information along the following lines: 'The piece you are going to hear now is called *The Dorian Horizon* . . . a leading Japanese composer of modern serious music. . . . He is generally held in high regard by critics of contemporary serious music.'

From the results of this experiment it is clear that those who heard the piece from the labelling bias of 'high status music' — that is to say, the group who were led to believe that it was from the area of progressive pop music — evaluated the music more favourably than those who thought the music originated from the contemporary 'serious' tradition, rooted in 'classical music'. The control group tended to be less extreme in their ratings and used the mid-points of scales, seeming to be somewhat adrift on the sea of evaluation without some kind of chart, or labelling system, to indicate how they might approach, describe and respond to what was, for them, a new musical experience.

Furthermore, Chapman and Williams found that, between the two main groups, descriptions of *The Dorian Horizon* were significantly wide apart on what they called a 'mood scale' (Joyful/ Sorrowful) and on a 'conventionality scale' (Weird/Normal). These scales of mood and conventionality would seem to correspond with what I have been calling expressive and structural elements and appear to measure, not so much levels of preference, but the way in which the music is actually perceived. There are then significant changes in perception as well as in value judgements, brought about by differences in prestige labelling. Taken with my own informal experiments with music graduates, this demonstrates that music is not approached with an 'innocent' ear but that our perception of it is conditioned by the value frame we bring with us.

Prejudice and valuing

It may now begin to seem that the various elements of the sequence of musical development and experience, whilst philosophically distinct, may be psychologically inseparable. If we take up a strong and inevitably limited value position, we may not even begin to attend to a particular musical performance, beyond sticking a particular category label on to it. Perception of expressive character and structural framing may never happen or, if it does, will be strongly conditioned by a particular set of expectations that are socially rather than musically generated. Within certain limits this appears to be so. There is a sense, though, in which music can be seen as objective, 'out there', to some extent independent of our particular preferences and prejudices. This is important, for it is in the autonomy of musical objects or events that education has some scope, a little room for manoeuvre. If we are to accept that what we perceive is totally shaped by what we believe, then we can neither teach nor learn. We might just as well be the mechanical inhabitants of a clockwork universe, where everything conforms to pre-specified rules.

Fortunately this is not so. As symbol makers and symbol users, we are able to contemplate alternatives to our belief systems, to put them to the test of evidence, to reconstitute our conceptual network. And there are such things as objective criteria which we acknowledge and rely upon in everyday life: these feed back into and shape our value systems.

To illustrate something of the relationship between the objective perception of things 'out there' and a subjective value response to them, an analogy might be helpful. Take, for instance, the way in which two people, Jack and Jill, might appear to agree or disagree about a third person, say a Giant. Jill might say that the Giant is huge, eats and drinks a lot, is noisy, a bit rough and ready and very extrovert. She might, being extrovert herself, thoroughly enjoy the company of the Giant and go to all his boisterous parties. Jack, on the other hand, might agree with Jill's description but not with her evaluation. Being of a reflective and scholarly disposition, he might find the Giant an overpowering bore and consequently try to avoid all invitations to his castle, preferring to spend his evenings more quietly. They each perceive similar features of the character of the Giant but differ in their value response. If either of them were to say that the Giant was a small, self-effacing and introverted person, he or she would be wrong, misinformed, or unobservant.

While it is true that Jack or Jill may, in describing the Giant, *emphasize* different aspects of his character, it is also true that there are limits beyond which we would be obliged to say that someone just did not *know* the Giant well enough to have a view about him. Any such opinion would be mere prejudice.

So it is with music. We would have to respect the judgement of someone who knew a particular piece of music very well but came to dislike it, just as we would accept the view of someone who really knew and admired music which we ourselves found unattractive. How different this is from dismissing out of hand or accepting without question whole categories of music.

This type of rejection or acceptance simply by looking at the label is not what I mean by valuing. The point is made in the DES 'Aesthetic development' document (1981) from the Assessment of Performance Unit. While I could not subscribe to the particular formulation and context of the statement (even as a member of the working group), yet there is some truth in it:

> It is important to distinguish between this [personal preference] and the valuing which is inseparable from artistic appraisals. Some personal preferences may be irrelevant to educated artistic appraisal, and may arise from, for instance, prejudice, or lack of understanding or experience. (p. 10)

There is indeed a distinction to be made between preferring or disliking something on the basis of direct acquaintance and accepting or rejecting things just because of the label under which they are packaged. Compare these two responses to the same recording of a pop song:

> This is the only group that can really sing,

and;

> The second song is a kind of noisy sound and I could listen to it for ever. There is a ringing sound in it which I seem to wait for.

Both of these statements were written by secondary school children I happened to be teaching and they are conceptually very different. The first takes as its starting place a value ticket, a label, the name of the group, and seems to be just a symptom of prejudice. The second comment appears to approach the state of valuing through a strong musical impression of the impact of sound materials in this specific song, hinting at a sense of structural expectation, and even perhaps revealing a degree of meta-cognitive self-observation in the introspective observation of a sound 'I seem to wait for'.

One way of dealing with prejudicial value systems — which can set like concrete around potential musical responses — is to avoid labelling altogether until the music has been really experienced. Music educators do well to follow the dynamic of the spiral and focus first on the way sounds behave and the necessary mastery of controlling them, along with encouraging the perception and articulation of expressive character and structural relationships; for it is on these elements of musical experience that real valuing is built.

It has to be acknowledged though, that the advertising and marketing industry will tend to reinforce the wearing of music as a badge, a signal, a slogan. Music under these conditions becomes *territorial*, owned. Writing in the *Independent* on 29 December, Dave Hill saw 1987 as the year when audiences became 'sects', a 'tribalism which increasingly characterizes the rock market as the turnover of fads gets faster'; surely not a new phenomenon. It is convenient and easy for those running the music market to divide audiences into various groups or clubs by appealing to exclusivity and the power of prestige. Purchasing music is then buying into a social group. Thus, an advertising bulletin for Country and Western exhorts me to buy records by a performer of this 'very special kind of music' and another advertisement asks us to 'thrill to virtuoso performances by Yehudi Menuhin, Elisabeth Schwarzkopf, and Maria Callas. And you'll discover a depth of enjoyment in music *that many people never find*' (my emphasis). One consequence of the exclusive nature of this form of cultural stereotyping is that birds of a feather will tend to flock together, as can be seen in the personal advertisements quoted by Murdoch and McCron in the *New Statesman* (1973):

Guy and Chick seek same, into Genesis, Cohen, Tolkien. No skins, peace, ta.

and

Scots skin wants bird, digs Slade, Reggae, Tamla.

Social position, age, family background, circles of friends and education, all have a part to play in determining the value positions from which music is regarded. No one is free to swim away from a whole raft of value assumptions which determine not only *what* music we can engage with but *how* we might respond to it.

Musical boundaries

All of these territorial systems — the mechanisms by which groups of people come to feel and declare their group identity and shared values — can only be maintained if music itself has easily identifiable features which signal to whom it 'belongs'. I would suggest that we could look again at the developmental/experiential spiral to see which elements of music communicate a sense of strong social boundary, enclosing a style within the territory of a particular cultural group, defined by age, race, gender, nationality or social class. These musical signals serve either to invite immediate acceptance or rejection — 'turn that rubbish off'. All that is needed is one phrase, sometimes a single bar or chord. We now have a tool with which to begin an analysis of these impediments to response and to begin to intervene educationally to positive ends. Consider the conditions under which music can alienate, or 'turn off' the would-be listener: these correspond with the first three modes of the spiral.

Music alienates people when they perceive:
a)   its sound materials as strange, or threatening;
b)   its expressive character to be strongly identified with another culture;
c)   its structure as either repetitive or confusing or aimless.

The impediment of new sounds

It is fairly easy to get used to a novel sound-spectrum, given enough exposure over a period of time. We notice how people fairly quickly adapt to electronically generated sounds, or to the folk instruments of South America or Africa, or to the scales of India or Arabia, or to an Indonesian or perhaps a Chinese orchestra; it is simply a matter of, so to speak, slightly retuning the 'ears'.

Educationally, this potential impediment is fairly easily overcome by repeated immersion until some of the novelty and strangeness of the sound wears off without conscious effort. Indeed, the natural and elemental interest in sounds as sensory experience can easily work to the advantage of the teacher; initially, novel sounds can be highly motivating. The exceptions might be when loudness levels are very high or the music is so continuous that it comes to be regarded as a form of aural pollution, intrusive. A more positive approach is simply to have students handle the materials of music for themselves, experimenting with various types of instruments, working with different scale and tuning systems, or building up some of the alternative sound worlds made possible electronically by the microchip.

The impediment of alien expressive character

Identification of expressive character, or musical gesture, with another cultural group can be a more serious obstacle, unless we already have some sympathy or at least a degree of tolerance towards the culture. There are instances of music which does not 'travel' too well around the cultural globe precisely because it is deeply embedded in 'local' ways of taking and making the world. We might think of medieval plainsong, of early punk rock, of eighteenth-century opera, of mid-European expressionism, of the Japanese Noh play. For some people, such mannered, highly stylized expressions of particular cultural groups are inaccessible, sometimes offensive. Even so, it is possible to counter prejudice to some extent, by trying to understand why and under what conditions the music comes to be made. It would, though, be better to work with culturally less embedded music, for example by avoiding currently partisan pop music, or extreme forms of operatic mannerism, or by taking musical procedures — the chord progression of the 12 bar blues, the technique of recitative, a twelve-note row — and working with them independently of their cultural origins and social labels, at least to begin with.

Expressive character is culturally the most powerful of the three elements, the most likely constituent of music to signal territorial or social exclusiveness. The psychological reason for this is clear: I have argued that musical expressiveness is a form of *imitation*, when we take on and to some extent become like someone or something other than ourselves; it is the point at which music touches 'real life', the world outside of itself. Because of this, musical gesture can be easily heard as 'belonging to' this or that group or life-style which we may happen to accept or reject. Jazz in the 1920s and 30s, heavy rock and drug-related forms of pop music are instances of this strong effect and have been seen from the outside the culture as immoral, destructive, unhealthy. Conversely, such socially powerful musics can be the focus for cultural identity and cultural solidarity; they become the anthems of cultural groups and the musical effect becomes amplified by labelling and cultural stereotyping, a process in which the media plays an active part.

The impediment of difficult structure

Even if we get over the strangeness of a new sound-spectrum and find the expressive gestures of music acceptable, there is still the potential barrier of structural conventions. The ability to 'read' musical norms requires some considerable experience and refinement of discrimination. It is no use listening to Mozart with Wagner 'ears', or to either composer expecting to hear musical organization along the lines of Genesis or Paul Simon. We get nowhere if we try to follow the *alap* of an Indian raga by listening for thematic 'development' in the manner of Beethoven or Brahms, or for the harmonic surprises of the Beatles. Again, a totally different set of structural expectations is implicit in the works of, say, Berio or Boulez, having much more to do with relationships and transformations between different sonorities than with metric, melodic or motivic norms and contrasts.

The role of the educator is to familiarize students with different structural conventions through active engagement — exploring and observing how musical ideas can become established and transformed through various ways of repeating and contrasting. Unlike expressive characterization, formal procedures are not so easily identified with particular cultural groups. The basic processes of repetition and contrast, with the derived devices of variation, transformation and re-positioning, are common across the musics of the world: their roots lie in the psychological universals of human perception, the ways in which we all seek to organize experience into meaning and coherence. I suspect that in music education we have only just begun to think about the teaching of musical structure, something that has precious little to do with all the books on 'form', which are very generalized abstractions of particular processes and sometimes tend to treat musical works as though they were actually written only to illustrate this or that musical procedure.

Removing the labels

It is neither true nor helpful to music education to assume with Graham Vulliamy and John Shepherd that everything about music is socially determined, culturally embedded (Vulliamy and Shepherd, 1984). If we believe that any musical tradition is able to be interpreted *only* through extra-musical references shared within a particular culture, then it follows that response to music will be a local phenomenon from which people of other cultures are largely excluded. If music is always so tightly woven into social structures and specific cultural practices, how can people possibly respond to the music of other times and places? Of course, some music does at certain times have this function and good examples would be *some* pop and rock, when it is employed as a signal of exclusive group identity or to promote transcendental anarchy. As Nik Cohn said of the Rolling Stones in a continuation of the quotation at the head of this chapter: 'The words were lost and the song was lost. You were only left with chaos, beautiful anarchy. You drowned in noise.'

Schools and colleges have no part to play in this. In music education, when the song is lost, all is lost. Through education, we look for the development of mind, for the aesthetic raising of consciousness not the anaesthesia of noise and physical catharsis, though these may have an important role elsewhere. Musical meaning is sufficiently abstract to travel across cultural boundaries, to step out of its own time and place. When music has become emotionally embroiled in local cultural practices or fads we would do well to avoid it in the curriculum, the song being for the while lost in the 'noise', either literally or metaphorically. Imagine the effect of the extreme anarchy of early punk rock in classrooms as part of a compulsory curriculum, or a determined music teacher wanting to sing Methodist hymns with classes consisting largely of Moslem children, however fine the words of Wesley might be. Most music, though, is not so tied down to cultural practice and is accessible to us if we give it a chance to speak.

To summarize: music can be culturally exclusive if the soundspectrum is strange, if expressive character is strongly linked with a particular culture or sub-culture and if structural expectations are inappropriate. All of these elements, especially expressive characterization, can be amplified by labelling and cultural stereotyping. The task of education is to reduce the power of such stereotypes through a lively exploration of musical procedures, phenomena which can be relatively independent of cultural ownership. This independence is the theme of the next chapter.

7

Music education in a pluralist society

> An emphasis on individual creators and performers, and a global view of the artistic conventions that they have used and use, are the surest means of developing the artistic consciousness of the nation. Such an enterprise will never succeed if it is multi*cultural*: it must be multi*artistic*. It can only be successful when people are touched by the aesthetic force of the arts and can transcend their social and cultural analogues.
>
> (John Blacking, *Culture and the Arts*: 18)

In the previous chapter I suggested that the territorial boundaries of music can be more closed than open, more or less culturally exclusive, depending on the context in which music originates, the use to which it is put and on the degree of cultural labelling attached by the media. So powerful is the image-making process that we tend to fall easily into stereotyping and media mythologies. Thus, through a study in Finnish upper-level primary schools, Leik Finnäs found that children fairly consistently overestimated the preferences of their peers for 'tough', 'wild', protesting, loud and rock-orientated music, underestimating preferences for classical and 'quiet' music. This effect was most marked when judging the preferences of a large, more anonymous peer group than when estimating the likings of their own classmates. It seems that an element of myth easily creeps into our perceptions of how others relate to music (Finnäs, 1987).

Relatively closed musical boundaries can be established on such a mythical basis, fencing out other people. Cultures can become cults. An example of this with Rap music in mind is given by Dave Hill in the *Independent* (29 December 1987):

102

Rap depends mightily on ornate processes of communion and confirmation, what with its specialized language, its endless responses and cross-references to other records, its rigorous adherence to dress codes and attitudes.

Within formal music education, that is to say, education run by institutions, it falls mainly to teachers to exercise the power of selection of musical idioms — *what counts as music*. Fundamentally, this is what lies behind the criticism offered to music educators by Graham Vulliamy and his co-writers. Music teachers, he maintains, have exercised this power by fencing off the idioms sanctioned by school and college, defining some musics negatively compared with the western classical tradition, seeing them as undeveloped, primitive or culturally inaccessible: first in respect of jazz, rock and pop, now with reference to other musical traditions, especially those of Africa and Asia (Vulliamy and Lee, 1976 and 1982). This is, or once might have been, generally so. To some extent music teachers may have been slow to come to terms with what were, for them, novel sound-spectra, with unfamiliar structural norms and especially with the distinctive, often earthy range of musical expression welling up from Afro-American sources, relatively free from notational constraints, improvised and rehearsed rather than composed and eventually performed by others. During our 1987 Gulbenkian-funded research, we certainly found some schools where music teachers never used jazz, rock or pop, or 'ethnic' music. (Even the unfortunate term 'ethnic', though generally understood and as yet unavoidable, gives the impression of higher and lower forms of music.)

Teachers, musicians and, until recently, western musicologists have tended to subscribe to cultural labelling, perhaps too easily believing certain idioms to be intrinsically inferior, or possibly undeveloped — a more compassionate if patronizing view — or, at least, none of their business. Certainly, many musics have been only lately admitted to *Groves* and the *New Oxford Companion to Music*. But such exclusiveness may just as easily be found in any strong tradition; among African master-drummers, Indian sitar teachers. Jazz musicians have been unwilling to accept rock and other forms of pop. Putting it relatively mildly, George Melly finds one of the defects of pop to be 'that it is essentially exclusive, tied only to the young and therefore incapable of development beyond a certain point' (Melly, 1970: 228).

There is a lot at stake if it is suggested that accomplished musicians should step outside of a well-developed idiom, leaving the relative security of hard-won special skills and finely tuned sensitivity. Teachers too cannot be expected to abandon those musical traditions in which they feel confident for poorly assimilated idioms from elsewhere. What then is our educational attitude and policy to what is sometimes called a 'multi-cultural society'? Can we be more positive?

Transcending cultures

If we are to catch hold of the vision of education that lies just round the corner from Blacking's challenging statement, that the aesthetic force of the arts can transcend their social contexts, then just a little more preparatory clarification seems necessary. A passage taken from the writing of the psychologist Jerome Bruner may help to focus in on what this transcendence is like and begin to identify the role of education in the transcendental process. Bruner tells us that:

> No human language can be shown to be more sophisticated than any other . . . but . . . it is in extracting from our use of language the powerful tools for organizing thought that people differ from each other . . .
>
> Less demanding societies — less demanding intellectually — do not produce as much symbolic embedding and elaboration of first ways of looking and thinking. Whether one wishes to 'judge' these differences on some universal human scale as favouring an intellectually more evolved man is a matter of one's values. But however one judges, let it be clear that a decision *not* to aid the intellectual maturation of those who live in less technically developed societies cannot be premised on the careless claim that it makes little difference.
>
> (Bruner, 1974: 66–7)

Schools in our society are an essential part, though only a part, of cultural intervention to aid intellectual development, to develop mind. By mind I do not mean to suggest some impoverished view of human mentality, resembling a calculating or reading machine; businesslike and efficient, commercially effective. The 'basics' of education are much more than this. Mind comprises the great networks of symbolic processes that human cultures have generated, sustained and refined through the ages: including the sciences, humanities and the arts, along with humour and sets of social conventions and ceremonies that facilitate conversation, mutual respect and sympathetic understanding. The true aim of education, as Bruner suggests, is consciously to fashion the tools for organizing thinking. Thought, as I tried to show much earlier, is not exclusively tied to a narrow range of cognition, nor to verbal language nor to systems of logical notation (such as those utilized by mathematics) which usually seek to condense and amplify what can be expressed verbally. We can *think* musically too.

Further insights into the culturally transcendental aims of education and schooling can be gleaned from the anthropological work of Margaret Mead. Here, while reminding us of the dangers of schooling, of the risks involved in the separation of education from its community basis, she offers a vision of formal education which we ought not to dismiss lightly.

> When we look for the contributions which contacts of peoples of different races and of different religions, different levels of culture and different degrees of technical development, have made to education, we find two. On the one hand, the emphasis has shifted from learning to teaching, from the doing to the one who causes it to be done, from spontaneity to coercion, from freedom to power. . . . But, on the other hand, out of the discontinuities and rapid changes which have accompanied these minglings of people has come another invention, one which perhaps would not have been born in any other setting than this one — the belief in education as an instrument for the creation of new human values. . . . the use of education for unknown ends.
>
> (Mead, 1942/1973: 107)

The problem of the loss of spontaneity and the corollary of institutional power are important matters to be addressed in the next chapter. For the moment though, is it possible to say a little more about these unknown ends? I think it is. John Blacking again, giving an account of his experiences among the Venda people, tells us that:

> although music making enabled people to express group identities and to experience social solidarity, its ultimate aim was to help them to pass beyond restricted worlds of culturally

defined reality, and to develop creative imagination.

(Blacking, 1985)

This is a striking observation and challenges any stereotype of 'tribal' music and dance as activities essentially locked into local and limited community values, though this is always a part of the story. What Blacking calls 'transcendental musical experiences' are not gained by staying within the confines of strong and socially embedded idiomatic traditions — the 'authentic' music of the tribe. It is by working with musical *processes* themselves as though they had a degree of autonomy that transcendence of these culturally restricted worlds becomes a possibility.

> Venda was one of many societies where people freely bor-
> rowed, adopted, and adapted songs, dances, ideas, and
> customs from others without anxiety about their cultural
> 'purity' . . .

It is here that we can begin to look for the essential role of formal education, for the particular contribution that schools and colleges can make. The songs people sing, the tunes they make, the dances they dance stem only partly from extra-musical cultural requirements and conventions. The materials and structure of musical instruments themselves fashion the tonal relationships of certain intervals and scales and particular rhythmic or timbre possibilities; in any culture musicians, given the slightest licence, will go beyond the immediate needs of ritual or community func-tion and decorate, elaborate, 'put bits in'; dancers will invent dance, not simply perform it, a fact evident even in discos. The secret lies in the human aspiration towards playful abstraction and the genera-tion of symbolic forms, such as language, mathematical thinking, music, dance and visual art. To bring this out I need to return just once more to Karl Popper and especially to his concept of self-transcendence.

> The incredible thing about life, evolution, and mental growth,
> is just this method of give-and-take, this interaction between
> our actions and their results by which we constantly trans-
> cend ourselves, our talents, our gifts.
> This self-transcendence is the most striking and important
> fact of all life and all evolution, and especially of human
> evolution.

In its pre-human stages it is of course less obvious, and so it may indeed be mistaken for something like self-expression. But on the human level, self-transcendence can be overlooked only by a real effort. As it happens with our children, so with our theories: we may gain from them a greater amount of knowledge than we originally imparted to them.

The process of learning, of the growth of subjective knowledge, is always fundamentally the same. It is *imaginative criticism*. This is how we transcend our local and temporal environment.

(Popper, 1972: 147)

When we remember that Popper admits music into his 'World Three' — the world of ideas, of logical relationships and theories, a world from which we all borrow and to which we all contribute; a world which we all to some extent *make*, as naturally and inevitably as spiders make webs — then we can begin to see what schools and other educational establishments should be doing: creating 'new human values' (Mead); extracting the 'powerful tools for organizing thought' (Bruner); promoting cultural 'transcendence' (Blacking); facilitating 'self-transcendence' and stimulating 'imaginative criticism' (Popper).

Music has its own ways of creating new values; transcending both self and immediate culture. Musical procedures can be absorbed and re-used over centuries of time, between vastly differing cultures and across miles of geographical space; they are not irrevocably buried in local life-styles, even though they may have birth there. Musical elements — that is to say, the sensory impact of sound materials, expressive characterization and structural organization — have a degree of cultural autonomy which enables them to be taken over and re-worked into traditions far removed from their origins. The fact that musical procedures can to some extent be freestanding, transferable, negotiable is vital to any sense of individual freedom, freedom to break out of the templates made by local cultures and our own personal repertoire of feeling and action. Without such scope, education is unthinkable, inconceivable.

Transformation and reinterpretation

Demonstration of how cultural products are constantly being

transformed and reinterpreted is not a difficult task; the ferment goes on all around us, asking only to be noticed. I shall give some musical examples but firstly will identify a fairly colourful instance of the process at work in verbal language. The exemplar of cultural transformation I have in mind is the adaptation of English vocabulary into New Guinea Pidgin, a language of great charm and potential humour and one which I happen to have been fortunate to see at work in its New Guinea context.

Melanese Pidgin has its origins in commercial interchange and there is no doubt that much of the vocabulary and grammar came into being through necessary negotiation with sailors putting into port with cargo, on ships arriving from Australia. During a working visit there in 1986, I was impressed by the manner in which certain facets of this language has been flexibly adapted to cope with the formalities of translation and the need for a written form.

My 'text' is taken from the translation of the biblical Psalms, published by the Bible Society of Papua New Guinea in 1979. For example, Psalm 70, verse 1, originally appears in the Cambridge 'Revised' version as follows:

Make haste to help me O Lord.

In New Guinea Pidgin we have:

Bikpela, Yu kam hariap na helpim mi.

The lexical origins of this are pretty obvious; the written form is more or less a phonetical notation of the aural experience we have of London Cockney and Australian 'bush', though the pronunciation of 'p' inclines towards that of an 'f'. The meaning soon becomes clear; there can be no misunderstanding, certainly not if we know the original source.
Again, take Psalm 71, verse 1:

In Thee, O Lord do I put my trust; let me never be confounded.

In Pidgin we get:

Bikpela, mi save stap wantaim yu (;) na ol birua I no inap bagarapim mi.

The literal translation of the second half would be something like:

And all violence (birua) is not enough (inap) to confound me.

The verb *to bagarup* is widely used to indicate any action when something is spoiled or broken. It is pronounced with a slightly rolled 'r', and is devoutly sung in churches, its linguistic origins happily of no great consequence.

Similar transformations ceaselessly take place in language and so they do in music. I give some examples almost at random. An English clergyman visiting Brazil sometime in the middle of the last century, describes the music played in church by the padre/organist:

> He had got, from a friend in Rio, some English music, consisting of country dances and marches, the names of which he did not comprehend; so he applied them to his church services, and it was with no small surprise we heard him begin his andante with 'the Duke of York's march', and conclude his allegro with 'go to old Nick and shake yourself'. This to us sounded exquisitely absurd and even profane, but it was not so to him or the rest of his auditors, who had formed no such association of ideas.
>
> (Source unknown)

From his account and from my own experience of Brazil, it is apparent that European military marches, fashionable dances and Viennese masses all travelled there in the nineteenth century, eventually to become resident and inspire local musicians to compose in similar styles. The polka, for example, seems to have begun life in rural Bohemia, turning up in Prague in the late 1830s. It was in Paris by 1840, London by 1844 and arrived in Brazil, probably via Portugal, shortly after. Now polkas can be found on tape and disc exemplifying the 'Brazilian' musical heritage along with recordings of church 'orchestras' (which include a choir). These orchestras are a feature of certain towns, notably São João del Rei, about three hundred and fifty miles from Rio. There, in beautiful Portuguese Baroque churches, they perform home-grown music, influenced by scores from Europe brought from Rio inland by mule during the first half of the nineteenth century, to be studied and emulated by local musicians who would probably never have been to an actual performance of the works which became their models.

I had the good fortune to sing with one of these 'orchestras' and know the strength of present-day commitment to this music. There is even a band room specially set aside for weekly rehearsals.

Other examples, again at random: the harmonic vocabulary of 'immoral' early jazz, complete with chromatic secondary sevenths, came largely from Victorian hymn books; the Jamaican Quadrille, though originating in the upper reaches of European society, has become assimilated into the folk traditions of the Caribbean, thanks to those slaves and servants in the great houses of the planters who observed the social antics of their superiors and were pressed into service to make up dance sets as required; Reggae owes quite a lot to American rhythm and blues (Cross, 1984). Recently on my travels, I came across a Papuan pop song which utilizes most of the ostinato from Pachelbel's *Canon* as a repeated bass and chord progression; not the first time that this serviceable progression has been put to work since its origins in seventeenth-century Nuremberg.

This musical traffic does not only run from west to east or north to south; nor does it only flow from 'classical' traditions to 'folk'. The drift is in all directions, unstoppable. Western 'symphonic' music (for want of a better term) has always absorbed elements from elsewhere like a great sonorous sponge. Haydn absorbed Slavonic turns of phrase; Debussy was impressed by the 'Cakewalk'; Stravinsky copied 'Ragtime'; Puccini did his homework on ancient Chinese turns for *Turandot*; Vaughan Williams soaked up model folk melodies from rural Britain; at some point, 'Moorish' dances became Morris dancing, hence the exotic costumes. In 1987, the composer George Benjamin heard people playing Peruvian flutes outside the Pompidou Centre in Paris; he invited the players inside and systematically recorded them playing all the sounds of which the flutes were capable. Eventually these recorded sounds were to be transformed and re-structured with other materials drawn from many differing sources, using the equipment of the *Institut de Recherche et Coordination Acoustique/Musique* to produce the commissioned work, *Antara*.

Similar transformations can be clearly discerned in punk rock. At its height anti-adult, anti-establishment and anti-authority, to many the music seemed brutal in sound spectrum, lacking in structural cohesion and definitely the territorial property of one social group, complete with dyed hair, scruffy clothes and assorted hardware shoved into the ears and nose. The whole phenomenon was amplified by cultural labelling, especially by the popular press.

Notice, though, that now that the cultural amplification has been switched off, the electronic amplification turned down and the dress conventions and musical tone of voice have lost some of their expressive and territorial charge, some of the elements of punk are more widely received, have been assimilated into the main cultural stream. Many a 'respectable' person of any age now leaves the hairdresser with a trace of dye and bristle; the products of reinterpretation and transformation. The same is also true of the musical elements of the era; they have filtered into the more general language of pop and rock as autonomous devices, carrying with them only a trace, just a flavour of their anarchic origins.

Whatever jazz musicians may have felt about this music and other forms of rock, some of the chord progressions and rhythmic 'feel' have been assimilated into the aural libraries of jazz improvisers. The point here is simply to stress the *autonomy* that cultural products can have, once they are freed from the chains of local cultural ownership, media labelling and territorial signalling. Time and use are able to unlock these chains and teachers would do best to avoid strongly culturally loaded idioms until their context has eroded, leaving behind what there is of musical value.

There is, of course, much more to cultural diversity than the issue of popular music. But pop is a good test case and has been the first alternative bundle of musical idioms to become fairly widely accessible to classroom practice within the framework of compulsory education in schools, just as jazz and rock have now been received respectfully into some of the most conservative institutions of higher education. The reasons for this lie fairly close to hand. Firstly, there has been fairly strong theoretical advocacy of the value of music from Afro-American sources; secondly, the social and subversive origins of jazz and of pop and rock have to a large extent been forgotten, leaving the music more free-standing and therefore more *musical*; thirdly, these idioms are pervasive, unavoidable. Even if music teachers have until recently not always participated in or consciously worked at the styles, at least they are aurally attuned to them through an unconscious process of osmosis.

There is no need to continue with a recitation of further examples: music is free to travel and, just like language, is continually being refashioned, adapted, reinterpreted — to create 'new human values', to 'organize thought', to 'transcend' the limits of local culture and personal self. Every new composition or improvisation is an act of transforming socially transmitted musical ideas into new expressions, inflecting and regenerating cultural heritages.

This dialectic process of taking and making music has already been identified in the development of children as they traverse the musical spiral from left to right — moving from the social sharing of manipulative control, to the commonplaces of vernacular conventions and more sharply focused idiomatic practices. All these are creatively transformed by idiosyncratic delight of direct sensory impression, unique personal expressiveness and imaginative structural speculation.

An inter-cultural attitude

We see then that musical procedures have some independence from social context. Music has a life of its own. The evidence for this lies in the obvious processes of reinterpretation and transformation: music from one time and place can be utilized elsewhere. Music is less accessible, though, when strong idiomatic boundaries are maintained. Idiomatic procedures are perceived as exclusive rather than inclusive when a sound spectrum seems strange, or when musical organization (structure) depends on unfamiliar norms, or when the expressive content is closely identified with a specific cultural group. In time the territorial origins of music lose their significance as musical processes themselves become accepted on their own terms.

The new challenge to music education comes from the musics of the south and east. Can these diverse styles be floated in the mainstream of music education? Should they be?

The answer to the first question is that they surely can be if we are prepared to regard them as music; not as ethnic or national flags or as exotic illustrations of a culture. This is why I prefer the integrative concept 'inter-cultural' to the more divisive and sometimes racist idea of 'multi-cultural'. It is discriminatory nonsense to say that we cannot understand something of, say, 'oriental' music without understanding oriental culture, the oriental 'mind'. To some extent the music *is* the culture. We enter the minds of others through what Popper would call their 'third world' products. We come to understand something of the ancient Greeks by looking at their pots and seeing their plays; more about the ancient Chinese by listening to and exploring their musical systems and medical practices. We get on the inside of jazz or rock by noticing and handling the chords and cadences; the modes and lyrics. Of course, there may be helpful things to know, bits of information

112

that help to set a context, but these are no substitutes for the direct experience of symbolic forms; in our case, making or taking music itself.

The answer to the second question is tied in with this and relates to our attitude to the accessibility of other musics. A range of styles should be experienced in education, not as 'examples' of other cultures, with all the stereotyping and labelling that goes with such an approach, but as objects and events carrying expressive meaning within a cohesive form.

Is it possible, though, to think of *all* music in this way or is such an aesthetic view a peculiarly western perspective?

> To the Western musician conciseness of expression, clearly shaped form, and individuality are the highest criteria by which a work of art is judged; the attitude of the listener is an active one: he likes to listen to what the composer has to say. The Eastern musician likes to improvise on given patterns, he favours repetition, his music does not develop, does not aim at producing climaxes, but it flows; and the listener becomes entranced by the voice of the singers, by the sound of the instruments, and by the drumming rhythms.
>
> (Wellesz, 1957: xviii)

Such immersion in music is certainly authentic and valid. Such a response is on the sensory plane of the experiential spiral, and may possibly be at expressive and structural levels. Expression does not need to be dramatic; it can be attitudinal, holding a steady musical posture without climaxes, or flowing organically on a stream of time. Structure is not always epigrammatic but can unfold on larger timescales, without tight punchlines. Nor do we need to attend to every detail of music; we can be occasional 'hearers' rather than continual 'listeners' and, at times, this would be the most appropriate and satisfying way to relate to music. Performances of the kind described by Wellesz can stretch out over days and nights, perhaps mingled with ritual or ceremony, with people coming and going, both attentionally and literally, as they might at an Indonesian shadow theatre, *Wayang Purwa*.

Experiences of this kind can be a most powerful educative force but they are not appropriate for classrooms. We might reverse this and say that classrooms may not be appropriate for these experiences. There has to be some analytical and critical talk in classrooms, some of it necessary, and bearing directly on music-making and musical perception. But in some cultures music is not so analysed or spoken of; in some African areas there is no word for music, though there is plenty of it. Merriam, in his classic study of the Flathead Indians, tells us:

> The Flathead *like* music; they view music as a proper and sometimes powerful part of the culture in which they live; they are on occasion moved by it and the structures in which it occurs; but they do not 'love' it with the verbalized passion of the aesthete.
>
> (Merriam, 1967: 46)

The verbalized passion of the aesthete seems to correspond with the mode of musical experience I have called valuing, perhaps with the systematic mode. There are, though, still questions of sound quality, manipulative control, expressive charge, vernacular and idiomatic authenticity: all the other elements of the spiral. Even among the Flathead, people discriminate within and appraise the music around them; they 'choose between good and bad singers, difficult and easy songs, personal and borrowed songs' (Merriam, 1967: 45). There is musical criticism. Similarly, Blacking tells us that Venda children were able to tell him when songs were right or wrong and to what purposes they were put (Blacking, 1984). This is a form of musical analysis. Among the great musical traditions of the Indian sub-continent, there is a strong element of critical and analytical discourse, even to the extent of aesthetic and psychological enquiry into the effects of music; reflection at the systematic level. Thus, expressive character is seen to be a function of mode colours which are also related to dramatic gestures — love and delight, laughter, sorrow, anger, heroism, fear, disgust and astonishment. Deriving from this experience of *raga* is 'rasa'.

> Rasa . . . is a sojourn in the inner world, an exploration of the unconscious; it is the aesthetic mode of transcendence, of quieting turmoil within and bringing it nearer to its perfect state of pure calm.
>
> (Kakar, 1978: 26–31)

This distinction between *raga* and *rasa* seems close to my own account of music meaning something 'to' us, its objective expressive character; and what music means 'for' us, the way in which it can permeate the essence of our thinking and feeling; the symbolic level of response (Swanwick, 1979).

Even the hard case, pop music, is not a candidate for uncritical acceptance: 'If popular music is to survive as anything more valuable than a source of revenue for innumerable merchants, it will require steady and purposeful criticism' (Palmer, 1976: 307).

Musical criticism at whatever level is crucial to the process of formal education. Imaginative criticism is the central and distinctive feature of courses in schools and colleges and such critical activity does not have to be on a high theoretical plane, but occurs whenever musical decisions are taken or music is thought or talked about. Brian Loane tells us that 'reflection on music made explicit and shared through verbal communication, is what constitutes music *teaching*' (Loane, 1984a: 34). Even the element of verbal communication may not be central; the idea of explicit insights that are demonstrated and shared in one way or another is what really matters. Hans Keller, when coaching a young string quartet, observed that one player shaped a certain phrase in a different way from another: 'Don't criticize in your playing', he said. Such criticism *within* music-making would indeed be inappropriate during performances, but *showing* someone else in rehearsal how a phrase might go rather than talking about it is a common enough feature of workshop practice. In the same manner we might try out a speed or instrumental effect during composition or performance, comparing it with an alternative or estimating its effectiveness, with or without much talk. Education is always a form of criticism; as distinct from either catharis, where we might achieve emotional release through group identity and immersion in noise; or training, when we accept some task as given and develop specific skills of articulation and control.

The aim of inter-cultural music education

The ultimate aim, then, of a music curriculum is not to transmit an arbitrary or limited selection of idiomatic values but to break out of 'restricted worlds of culturally defined reality' and promote 'imaginative criticism', bringing procedures and criteria out into the open. A formal music curriculum has a major role to play in making musical processes *explicit*. This attitude of cultural and self-transcendence can be initiated and sustained at any level of age and maturation. There are certain questions that recur: How does this work? Could it be different? How do other people deal with it? What might we learn from them? Can it be improved? In this way the human species preserves the power of adaptation.

Teachers cannot be expected to be *skilled* in all the musics of the world, but they must be *sensitive* to many and skilled in at least one. Musical sensitivity arises out of receptive attention coupled with an understanding of the *universality* of musical practice and a recognition that idiomatic variations arise out of a common human theme, best rendered as a verb, an impulse 'to music'. By working through performance, composing and in audience to the music of others, the potential range of idiomatic experience is limitless.

A music curriculum that is truly pluralistic might best be generated by identifying 'sets of sound' in a progressive sequence, linking these to specific musical encounters drawn from across different musical cultures, always chosen for their sonorous, expressive and structural impact. These 'sets of sound', consisting of intervals, scales, ragas, chords, note-rows, ostinati, drones, and so on, would be explored and transformed inter-culturally through composition, audition and performance (Swanwick and Taylor, 1982). This can be organized by working through the developmental spiral. For example: children in the upper years of a junior school might handle a pentatonic scale, first exploring the series as a special kind of sound collection (sensory); then controlling, perhaps copying *ostinati* or echo phrases (manipulative); then inventing a piece of their own perhaps with a title (personal expressiveness); then as an accompaniment to a known song (vernacular); and finally as a basis for a composition which has to have contrasting material (speculative). The range of idiomatic encounters can be extended through the use of recordings; after all, pentatonic scales are in use from China to Scotland.

By the end of eleven years of compulsory schooling, it would seem reasonable for students to have developed a sketch map of world music, some idea of where music can be found and how it 'goes'. Michael Webb, a colleague who was teaching in Papua New Guinea, suggests that studies in their provincial high schools should involve music from the following areas:

a) South Pacific — Melanesia, Micronesia, Polynesia and Australia
b) Asia — India, Japan, Indonesia

c) Africa
d) Europe — Middle Ages, Renaissance, Baroque, Classical Romantic, twentieth century
e) Americas — South and North

This is an ambitious inter-cultural programme and we are as yet nowhere near realizing anything so far-reaching. Nor can we, unless we are prepared to be much more systematic in building up a curriculum spanning eleven years in a less haphazard way than is presently the case. Even then, we must not pretend that we can do it all, that schools offer a comprehensive education.

Education in classrooms, especially school classrooms — the compulsory element of the educational system — will inevitably be limited in scope and function and especially in the depth of experience. What schools can never do is suspend the exercise of what Small calls conscious knowledge. They are unlikely places for dreaming, or for 're-establishing contact with the totality of mental life' (Small, 1977: 226-7). The strength of schooling lies, as Margaret Mead, Blacking, Popper and Bruner remind us, in the possibility of the creation of new values, in transcending culture, in critical reflection, going beyond 'first ways of looking and thinking'.

Imaginative criticism is the special task of formal education: bringing ideas to consciousness, asking questions, probing, trying things out. In one sense this goes beyond and yet at the same time is more limited than the more natural and communal processes of enculturation — learning simply by being there. Freer, less fragmented and perhaps more profound responses to music belong to other times and places. What happens in classrooms should, though, help to equip us to dream and synthesize elsewhere; but this is the focus of the following chapter.

Beyond the classroom

There is, though, much more to education than classrooms, as Christopher Small argues.

When one considers a school, college or university and the resources of skill, knowledge and experience it contains (itself only a tiny fraction of the community's store of skill and knowledge which is waiting to be drawn upon) one greatly regrets that only a tiny, arbitrarily chosen, sector is accessible to any individual student; the rest, if he is aware at all of its existence is put out of his reach by the demands of the syllabus and of examinations.

(Small, 1977: 187)

Much musical experience will certainly take place outside of classrooms and will be unconstrained by any kind of formal syllabus. There is a second role to be played within the formal system of music education. Music extends beyond classrooms into the social fabric of schools and colleges as educational communities, and into the world outside. The formal system has a part to play in organizing such specific elective activities as choirs, brass bands, jazz, folk and pop groups, 'musicals', and so on. The school or college, though, is only *one* agency promoting music in the community. This programme of events does not therefore need to be comprehensive, nor could it be.

In an important sense, educational institutions should be 'clearing houses', where students can find information about and have experience of the richness of musical possibilities 'out there'. This function of mapping out and giving access to the vitality of musical events would have to be developed much more than it presently is; drawing on multifarious formal and informal agencies — churches, temples, regional arts associations, local music groups and so on. Taking students out to musical events and bringing musicians in is a powerful educative force, even if it does sometimes cause administrative problems. A word of caution though: when there is strong identification of musical activities with particular groups inside and outside of schools, whether religious, political or ethnic, there must be *choice*: mandatory participation runs the risk of becoming cultural indoctrination.

In short: the first and unique aim of music education in schools and colleges is to raise to consciousness and purposefully and critically explore a number of musical *procedures*, experienced directly through the reality of various inter-cultural encounters. A second aim is to participate in creating and sustaining musical events in the community, events in which people can *choose* to be involved and thus contribute to the rich variety of musical possibilities in our society.

In these ways, we avoid transmitting a restrictive view of music and of culture and may help to keep prejudice at bay. Human culture is not something to be merely transmitted, perpetuated or preserved but is constantly being re-interpreted. As a vital element of the cultural process, music is, in the best sense of the term, *re-creational*: helping us and our cultures to become renewed, transformed.

8

Instruction and encounter

The outward and visible sign of the subject is the syllabus,
a table of contents which lays down what the student is
required to do and on what he is examined. . . . The syllabus
narrows the student's vision at the edge of knowledge and
cuts him off from precisely those fuzzy areas at the edges of
subjects that are the most interesting and rewarding.
(Christopher Small, *Music – Society – Education*: 186–7)

The moral of this fable is that if you're not sure where
you're going, you're liable to end up someplace else.
(Robert Mager, *Preparing Instructional Objectives*: Preface)

Once music-making and music-taking is abstracted from everyday
cultural life and becomes institutionalized in schools and colleges,
questions have to be faced not only as to *what* music is included
or excluded but *how* teaching and learning is to be managed.
Through the processes of curriculum selection and the organization of learning, institutions become notorious makers and
guardians of boundaries. They maintain their own sub-cultures by
means of rules, social order, age and sometimes gender specification and, most powerfully of all, through the ways in which
knowledge is structured. What counts as knowledge is defined by
schools, colleges and examination systems. Outside of these institutions, different cultural groups maintain their own codes and belief
systems, defining what is thought to be worthwhile or 'good',
marking out territory and boundaries. Music is often brought into
service for these purposes. Within institutions, what is worth
knowing is similarly classified and framed.

Classification and framing

The concepts of *classification* and *framing* are not new and were first developed in the work of sociologist Basil Bernstein (1971). They are helpful here, serving as a reminder of the power and control that schools and colleges exercise over the selection of knowledge and its transmission. Classification has to do with the exercise of selection over curriculum content, the way in which certain activities, perhaps 'subjects', are marked out for inclusion in or exclusion from the curriculum. The territorial boundaries of music are a classification system. A teacher selecting only music from the western classical traditions for inclusion in the classroom, would be working to relatively closed musical boundaries, strong rather than weak classification. Weak classification would give room for student decisions about curriculum content; in musical terms, this may include choice of idiom.

Framing, a different but related concept, is to do with pedagogy, teaching style, with the degree of control that the teacher or student possesses over selection, organization and pacing of what is to be learned. Strong framing is most easily identified with formal instruction, work that is teacher directed. Weak framing leaves more scope for decisions on the part of students as to how, when and, to some extent, what they will learn; a pedagogy or teaching style more committed to choice for individuals.

These are important distinctions well brought out by Margaret Mead. Reflecting on her anthropological work on Manus Island, she draws out some of the contrasts between the Islanders' implicit concept of education and the then current educational practice in the USA (Mead, 1942). She identifies a change from spontaneous choice to institutional coercion, from 'freedom to power', where the emphasis 'has shifted from learning to teaching'; what Bernstein might call a move towards strong classification and framing.

> There are several striking differences between our concept of education today and that of any contemporary primitive society; but perhaps the most important one is the shift from the need for an individual to learn something which everyone agrees he would wish to know, to the will of some individual to teach something which it is not agreed that anyone has the desire to know.
>
> (Mead, 1942/1973: 98)

In order to see classification and framing at work in music education, we could try placing some 'for instances'. For example, running a church choir preparing for a traditional carol service involves strong idiomatic classification — only certain types of music would be acceptable; *and* strong framing — the teacher is likely to function as a 'director of music' rather than a facilitator of individual discovery. We might come to a similar conclusion about a music class lesson in a school, where a teacher has decided to undertake a classroom rehearsal of, say, the chords of the 12-bar blues: once again, strong classification and framing. In both of these settings the teacher exercises considerable power over the idiomatic content — what counts as music — along with control over the pacing and mode of learning. If the work on the 12-bar blues was individualized, with the teacher acting as enabler and adviser rather than instructor, then we might describe this as strongly classified as far as musical idiom is concerned but more weakly framed. This is important: strong or weak classification does not always imply a similar emphasis in framing; there are two concepts here, not one. Any music education event could be placed somewhere within these two dimensions, though in flexible teaching there may be considerable movement between the extremes of weak and strong.

Figure 7: Curriculum classification and framing (after Bernstein, 1971)

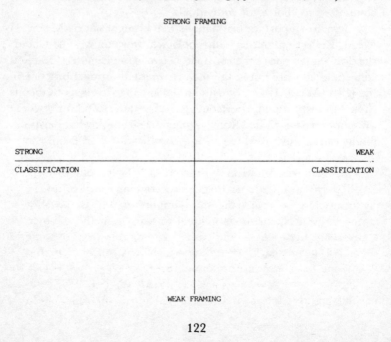

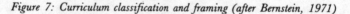

For instance, when someone *asks* how to balance a canoe, or drive a motor car, or finger a guitar, then strong framing may be desirable, necessary and expected. But under these conditions there is an element of 'student' *choice* as to what knowledge is appropriate; he or she has made a decision on classification, what is to be learned, and initiates contractual arrangement with the teacher who will decide on the framing. The problem with formal education in purpose-designed institutions is that this contract may be made indirectly with other agents than the student him- or herself; perhaps with a parent. In our schools, a degree of classification is now enshrined in the laws of the country. Beyond this, the detail of curriculum content and teaching method — what actually takes place is still most frequently left to individual teachers to decide. Even when the learning initiative is handed over to small groups, perhaps engaged in composing, dominant students will tend to influence both classification and framing by the strength of their ideas and force of personality. This is natural and inevitable. As Brian Davies reminds us, the social *is* control.

> One does not choose to live without rules and their consequences, though, at times and in some degree it is possible to choose which rules to live with. To know this is to be freer than not to know it.
>
> (Davies, 1986: 7)

Schools are committed to organize or frame education in some form or other; they are not merely social groups where informal enculturation takes place, but have an ethical and contractual responsibility for the development of *mind*. The obligation to frame knowledge is therefore inescapable, though pupil discovery or encounter might be built into this process.

In the previous chapter I emphasized the importance of *choice* whenever music education moves within strongly classified idioms. Here, I want to explore the effect of framing on music teaching, substituting for strong framing the term *instruction* and for weak framing the more affectively charged word, *encounter*.

Musical instruction

One outstanding characteristic of instruction is the tendency to specify behavioural or performance objectives. The debate about behavioural objectives has gone on for many years on both sides of the Atlantic, those arguing in favour including Mager (1975) and Bloom et al. (1964) and those against represented by Eisner (1985) in the USA and Stenhouse (1975 and 1978) in Britain. The arguments for and against such a model of educational transactions are well rehearsed by their advocates and it is necessary here only to pick out the essentials for the purpose of clarification.

Fundamentally, says Mager, a teacher is required to differentiate between the *activity* taking place in a classroom or studio and what is actually *learned*. Essentially, what is learned is that which remains with the student when the activity is over, perhaps in the form of some change of knowledge, attitude, understanding or skill. For example, we might practise improvising on a 12-bar blues chord sequence and may become fairly proficient at this. This proficiency does not vanish when we stop playing but forms part of the basis of our next engagement with the sequence. We carry learning with us when the activity is over; 'a child should emerge from a lesson a little altered' (Salaman, 1983: 6). This is a very salutary concept for any teacher: just *occupying* people is not the same as assisting in their education. Music lessons surely have to be more than just *doing* things.

Another fundamental characteristic of instructional objectives is that the learner should demonstrate what learning has been acquired and that teachers are able to identify what these signs of learning might be. The classic formulation, given by Mager, is to specify not only the *behaviour* that demonstrates the learning, but the *conditions* under which the demonstration or 'performance' of this learning might take place, along with the *criteria* to be used for judging the level of performance that would be acceptable. To give a fairly limited musical example: a teacher may have decided that among the required signs of some comtence in aural development will be that students recognize and name six musical instruments played on tape or record (the behaviour). They should be able to do this when at least three instruments are heard in combination (the conditions). An acceptable level of achievement (the criterion) might be that at least five of the instruments should be named correctly. Having formulated these instructional objectives, the teaching strategy can then be decided.

Another example might be in the context of a rehearsal, where a brass band conductor expected the euphonium player to hold his or her line (the behaviour), in time with the others during a particular piece played at a steady speed (the conditions), with no mistakes and consistently phrased (the criteria).

Whole programmes of music education have been built up from the premise that it is possible to specify as behavioural objectives what is required of the student, especially in the USA and more recently in connection with the British GCSE. One great advantage is that assessment is built into the procedure of specifying instructional objectives.

The very idea of objectives, or 'benchmarks' of this kind, carries along with it two fundamental implications: the first of these is that it is actually possible to identify the 'behaviours' that would demonstrate that learning had actually taken place; the second is that these 'behaviours' can be predicted in advance. Both of these crucial assumptions are open to question and will be challenged later. Some of the contentious features of behavioural objectives are fairly easily countered, as can be seen if we consider a few of the objections before centring in on the major problems.

One obvious worry is that formulating objectives trivializes the activity; focusing our attention on those things which can be easily observed, distracting us from more important but less obvious outcomes. So, for example, we may notice how well pupils can technically manipulate an instrument or whether they sing in tune but in so doing miss important things, such as sensitivity or appreciation. The disciple of the objectives school will answer that the fine details of teaching and learning are always, in a sense, trivial. In order to motivate the student there must be a sense of achievement, mastery over quite small details. As for such ideas as sensitivity or appreciation, these are vague terms, capable of many interpretations; belonging with other *being* words, such as 'understand', 'value', 'enjoy', 'be committed to', 'respond to' and 'use imagination'. The kind of educational language favoured by those who work to objectives would consist of much sharper *doing* words; for example, that students should be able to list, classify, apply, contrast, differentiate, compare, contrast, identify, demonstrate and produce.

Another common objection to behavioural objectives concerns the loss of flexibility. What about those unpredicted opportunities that might arise when teaching; unexpected changes of direction which may be significant and relevant for the student and make the whole experience more exciting, delving into what Small calls those fuzzy areas at the edges of subjects? The answer to this would be that we can simply reformulate and change objectives, substituting one set for another, not abandoning the procedure altogether. It is, after all, important to start with something like a sense of direction. If we were to achieve alternative objectives, fair enough. If there were outcomes over and above those already specified then this would be a bonus on top of a steady income.

A further worry might be that the formulation of behavioural objectives is undemocratic, in the sense that students have no say in the classification and framing of knowledge. One answer to this might be that objectives are public declarations of what is intended. They are not hidden away subversively or camouflaged in woolly and undefined words such as 'sensitivity' or 'imagination'. Because they are public they can be negotiated and changed, perhaps in consultation with the students.

It might be said, though, that activities such as music, which is after all an art, are much more difficult to teach through the use of objectives than, say, mathematics or science. It may be that we do not know what the outcome of an artistic activity might be: for example, what would be the outcome of setting a small group a task of composing a piece called 'Darkness'? Is the outcome really predictable? If so, then where is the element of originality and creativity in artistic or musical production? An answer to this is to question whether it is really true that we have *no* idea of what counts as original and creative. If we really are so ignorant and unaware, we may wonder about our ability as teachers to respond to what students do.

There remains a strong suspicion that the formulation of objectives *before the event* tends to drive out the magic of music and the spontaneity that enlivens human relationships. It is indeed an open question as to whether the *prediction* of objectives is essential or whether we should not rather be prepared to recognize achievement when it actually *occurs*, thinking in terms of learning outcomes rather than objectives. There is certainly no need to focus only on the mechanical aspects of skill or the informational aspects of knowing about music, rather than those other elements which comprise musicality and which appear in the developmental spiral. In an earlier attempt to raise the level of objectives to include those things which seem important to musicians, the following general categories were developed.

The student should be able to:

a) recognize and produce in music a range of expressive gesture;
b) identify and display the operation of structural elements;
c) demonstrate aural discriminations, technical fluency, use of notations;
d) assemble and categorize information about music and musicians.

(Swanwick, 1979: 67)

As it stands, such a formulation requires some explanation, especially of expressive gesture and structural elements. These were, in fact, the central concerns of that particular book and have been further developed in the earlier chapters of this one. Even so, it is still difficult to objectify the valued and powerful 'peak experiences', that are often reported as a feature of musical response. We might notice in a student a strong level of commitment to music, perhaps manifested in the 'behaviour' of buying recordings of Sting, or shouting 'bravo' at the opera, or asking to use a practice room; though these signs by themselves will never adequately reveal to us the internal feeling-state of the observed person and it would be presumptious to assume that they could.

One advantage of approaching curriculum practice from the standpoint of instruction through behavioural objectives is that it shifts the focus of teachers towards the behaviour of students and the detail of the activity. The charisma of the teacher defers to the performance of the student. The major hazard of regimenting learning through a predetermined sequence of fixed objectives is that little scope may be left for significant *encounters*, during which people respond in their own way, framing educative experiences for themselves. When most of the control of learning lies with the teacher, the student may not be able to make it his or her own, and the whole transaction can become stale and arid.

Musical encounters

Amongst the Venda, Blacking tells us, music is learned in the context of other social activities — informally from peers; by trial and error preceded by observation and listening; without graduated learning; joining in with music and gradually getting it right (Blacking, 1984). Above all, music is a social art, where playing with and listening to others is the motivation, the experience and the learning process. This is music education by *encounter*. Music is not dissected into little bits for the purpose of practice or analysis but presented and taken as a whole in a total social context. Consequently, the musical experience of the participants is multi-layered, rich in possibilities and certainly not sequentially organized in order of difficulty. Because of this, each 'learner' can choose his or her own speed of learning and, to some extent, the things which will be learned on any single occasion. Music experience within such a context of community events has no need for curriculum justification, being clearly valued by people of all ages and tribal status. There is no need for Venda people to argue for music curriculum resources or for their political leaders to demand better educational results, more efficient teaching. Graded exercises, sequential steps, programmed learning, instructional objectives, musical analysis and formal assessment procedures are of no consequence here.

Reading Blacking's description of the way in which the Venda learn music, I am reminded of my own experience as a boy in a Midlands village brass band. Music was to some extent learned in the context of other social activities: we knew that we would be playing at Remembrance Day services or garden parties or on parade at other village events. I mastered the technique of the E flat tenor horn informally, without instruction — the band master never quite got round to *instruction*. Most of the playing was of whole pieces or long sections with very little fragmentation into part-learning or analysis of particular difficulties. In fact, Blacking's description of the Venda fits perfectly: 'The main technique of learning was by observation and listening, trial and error, and then frequent rehearsal'. It was also considered vital to be playing with others. Few members of the band seemed to practise at home very often or for long and most technical progress seemed to be achieved mainly when playing together. I suspect that this pattern of learning is still prevalent today in church choirs, amateur orchestras, rock bands, folk groups, the Salvation Army, steel bands and many other variations of our rich musical culture.

Encounter-based music education of this kind contrasts quite sharply with musical instruction: scales and exercises; slow practice; graded pieces; a 'progressive' instrumental examination system; 'one hand at a time'; individual practise; learning programmes on the computer; the Kodály Choral Method and the sequential classroom syllabus of the American high school band.

The world of instruction may seem daunting and less convivial

128

than this domain of encounter, though we must be careful not to make the simplistic assumption that instruction is inevitably linked with high standards while encounter carries with it the suggestion that 'anything goes'. Blacking reminds us that excellence was applauded by and sought among the Venda, though it was clearly *acquired* in a different way from working through exercises on the theory of music or undergoing courses of individual tuition in dance or drumming. We notice here that the 'content' of music education as described by Blacking tends strongly towards the right-hand side of the Swanwick and Tillman spiral: there is admiration of manipulative skills, and a strong emphasis on initiation into both the general vernacular and the particular idioms of the community. This undoubted musical ability develops not through formal teaching processes but by encounter, one of the most effective 'mixed-ability' teaching strategies that could be devised. The Venda seem to be a good example of enculturation rather than formal education, learning things of unquestioned traditional value (strong classification) in informal ways (weakly framed).

Encounter and the curriculum

From the earliest beginnings of music education there are elements of response which are not amenable to instruction, let alone the prediction of objectives. The spiral of musical development helps to draw these out. For example, it is not easy to predict and impossible to 'instruct' the student in the impact of the sensory qualities of an instrument. I can remember the excitement brought on by the sounds that came out of the E flat horn when I first tried to play it; and even the very smell of resin or the musty odours of a brass or woodwind instrument that has been locked away in a case for some time have a strong sensory magic, let alone the sounds they might make.

By school age, children are almost certainly highly sensitive in their individual ways to expressive gesture in music and many will be moving towards appreciating speculative elements; structural tensions and resolutions, various forms of contrast and surprise; perceptions made possible through an accumulation of musical expectations. It would indeed then be an error to concentrate on what Stenhouse calls 'skill in a straightforward sense', insensitive to aspects 'of personal interpretation' (Stenhouse, 1975/1978: 81). It may, though, be helpful to do so *sometimes* in order to analyse and resolve a particular problem. So, a string teacher might recognize that the breakdown of a piece in performance is caused by some awkward fingering. It might at that stage be important to formulate a behavioural objective — that the student should be able to finger the passage in such a way as to make it manageable — for the time being suspending attention to other elements of musical response: *but only for the time being.*

Stenhouse is emphatic in his belief that higher levels of learning are not to be managed through schemes of objectives. He places upon the teacher the task of continual refinement of 'a philosophical understanding of the subject he is teaching and learning, of its deep structures and their rationale' (Stenhouse, 1975/1978: 91). It is just this *deep structure* of music which has motivated my own quest for a developmental and critical model; an analysis of what musical experience really *is*, what happens when people relate to music. The effective teacher is sensitive to the needs of students and to the structure and nature of the subject.

The need to develop musical criteria is nowhere more apparent than when children are composing, for here, as when writing an essay, the unexpected and the unpredicted mark out the most telling work. A musical composition that is totally predictable fails to meet the criterion of structural interest, is psychologically weak and will lose our attention beyond the first few minutes. It will certainly not stand up to repetition. We noticed this in the compositions of children. Until the speculative element involved in the effective handling of musical structure begins to appear, pieces either lack coherence or are devoid of any element of surprise, even though they may be quite strongly characterized in terms of mood, atmosphere or gesture.

A teacher coming across such work will bring to it an analytical, critical edge and might ask for some form of contrast or transformation, some element of deviation from repeated vernacular commonplaces. The essential elements of helpful response are the integrity of the judgemental criteria and the sensitivity of the teacher as music critic, for formal music education is, inevitably, *musical criticism.* The effectiveness and insightfulness of this criticism derives substantially from the quality of the teacher's own musical encounters and the ability to reflect upon them. If critical discourse is to be developed and sustained beyond the elementary, some analysis of what music *is* must take place. Hence the main themes of this book.

Tacit knowing

The fundamental difference between musical encounter in the community and music education in schools and colleges is precisely the obligation of evaluation and criticism, of becoming *explicit*, which is characteristic of formal settings. To what extent education at a deep level can ever be explicit is really the crucial problem of schooling, especially where the arts are concerned. The issue seems to resolve itself down to the beautifully simple but profound statement by Polanyi in *The Tacit Dimension* (1967), when he says '*we can know more than we can tell*'.

Much of life goes by on the basis of what Polanyi calls tacit knowing. For example, we *know* the face of a friend though we may never have itemized and described the features. Even after years of acquaintance we may not be able to say what colour his or her eyes may be or how far apart they are, whether the cheek bones are high or low. In order to do this we would have to resort to something like the technique of the police when they try to get an identi-kit description from a witness in order to *tell* others how the suspect actually looked. In music, we may be impressed by a general quality of movement or ongoingness, or of a particularly strong stylistic flavour but may be only tacitly aware of all the melodic, rhythmic, and instrumental details that contribute towards the total impression that we form. They are all heard in combination, as a *whole*, and any analysis down into smaller-than-the-whole implies that we must, for the time being, abandon our focus on the totality of the experience, which is its most satisfying and significant quality. Polanyi takes a position in a famous passage which challenges the behavioural objectives model at its very foundations.

> if we know a great deal that we *cannot tell*, and even if that which we know and *can* tell is accepted by us as true only in view of its bearing on a reality beyond it, (an indeterminate range of unsuspected results) . . . then the idea of knowledge based on wholly identifiable grounds collapses, and we must conclude that the transmission of knowledge from one generation to the other must be predominantly tacit.
>
> (Polanyi, 1967: 25)

Presumably, telling may include showing; not all communication will be through the spoken word. When students compose and perform they are *showing* what they know even if they are not literally telling us. The problems really arise when people are *in audience* to music, a difficulty carefully analysed by Brian Loane (1984a). The need for critical conversation is especially apparent when trying to share a listening experience with others or helping to develop musical sensitivity and insight. Following Polanyi, Reese suggests that when students are placed in an audience role, they should always first encounter the work without analysis or talk (Reese, 1980). Only then might they begin some form of analysis and ultimately should be left alone with the music, not listening *for* such details but listening *through* them.

What students have to say or 'tell' about this experience is important. Although what can be said will always be partial and provisional, such discourse will be an essential part of teaching and learning. Sensitive musical criticism has the power to enhance musical response. Ultimately though, we must each of us be left alone, as Polanyi himself made clear in a discussion of music, saying that 'the sensory quality which conveys this content cannot be made explicit. It can only be lived, can only be dwelt in' (Polanyi and Prosch, 1975: 34).

Two examples from music education

Consider the following collection of maxims. The first list comes from Murray Schafer, and appears at the beginning of the *Rhinoceros in the Classroom* (1975). The second, with a coincidentally similar title, comes from Mrs Curwen, part of the Preface to her *Pianoforte Method* (1886). Almost ninety years separate these two declarations and there is a difference in cultural perspective; Murray Schafer, a composer living in Canada in the twentieth century, and Mrs Curwen, an influential piano teacher in Victorian England. But let them speak for themselves.

MAXIMS FOR EDUCATORS

Above my desk I have written some maxims for educators, to keep myself in line. They are these:

1. The first practical step in any educational reform is to take it.
2. In education, failures are more important than successes. There is nothing so dismal as a success story.
3. Teach on the verge of peril.

4. There are no more teachers. There is just a community of learners.

5. Do not design a philosophy of education for others. Design one for yourself. A few others may wish to share it with you.

6. For the 5-year-old, art is life and life is art. For the 6-year-old, life is life and art is art. This first school-year is a watershed in the child's history: a trauma.

7. The old approach: Teacher has information; student has empty head. Teacher's objective: to push information into student's empty head. Observations: at outset teacher is a fathead; at conclusion student is a fathead.

8. On the contrary a class should be an hour of a thousand discoveries. For this to happen, the teacher and the student should first discover one another.

9. Why is it that the only people who never matriculate from their own courses are teachers?

10. Always teach provisionally: only God knows for sure.

(Schafer, 1975)

A FEW EDUCATIONAL MAXIMS

Showing the Principles on which the Method of the *Child Pianist* is founded.

1. Teach the easy before the difficult.
2. Teach the thing before the sign.
3. Teach one fact at a time, and the commonest fact first.
4. Leave out all exceptions and anomalies until the general rule is understood.
5. In training the mind, teach the concrete before the abstract.
6. In developing physical skill, teach the elemental before the compound, and do one thing at a time.
7. Proceed from the known to the related unknown.
8. Let each lesson, as far as possible, rise out of that which goes before, and lead up to that which follows.
9. Call in the understanding to help the skill at every step.
10. Let the first impression be a correct one; leave no room for misunderstanding.
11. Never tell a pupil anything that you can help him to discover for himself.
12. Let the pupil, as soon as possible, derive some pleasure from his knowledge. Interest can only be kept up by a

sense of growth in independent power.

(Curwen, 1886)

I notice that Mrs Curwen takes a systematic and sequential approach to what she does, teaching the easy first, the usual before exceptions, proceeding from the known to the unknown. Unlike Murray Schaffer, she has a view as to what is 'correct'. Schafer seems to reject this explicit model of instruction, putting forward a view of music education as encounter. Everything is provisional; there appears to be no continuity; nothing is 'correct'; there is no identifiable subject matter, or even a set of criteria, so far as one can tell. Words like 'failures', 'dismal', 'peril', 'fathead' and 'trauma', reveal his distrust of what I have been calling formal education. We are urged always to teach provisionally since there is no certainty in anything. Against this, Mrs Curwen believes that it is possible to teach *something* and she seems fairly sure as to what this something might be.

Both writers communicate a strong sense of respect for the pupil. Both acknowledge the virtue of 'discovery'. For Mrs Curwen, pupils should never be told anything they can discover for themselves, while for Murray Schafer, a class should be an hour of 'a thousand discoveries'. Both seem to agree that a sense of *encounter* is essential, for that is implicit in the very idea of discovery — propelling ourselves at our own speed towards the, as yet, unknown. The difference lies in the assumptions each of them make about what waits to be discovered. We can be fairly sure that Mrs Curwen knows pretty well what the student will find, whereas Murray Schafer would probably insist that discoveries, by definition cannot be predicted or known in advance by the teacher. Mrs Curwen has enough respect for 'a sense of growth in independent power' to be wary of discovery 'by numbers', and I can imagine her delightedly sharing in the discovery of a chord; or that one of the piano pedals helps to create a kind of musical fog; that a melody still exists even though it be disguised. But she will be predicting the sequence of learning in a firmer way than Murray Schafer; framing knowledge more strongly, leading the student firmly on.

What really marks out the nineteenth-century pianist-teacher from the twentieth-century composer-teacher is her certainty of curriculum *content*, strong classification. Schafer inhabits a world where musical styles and musical language have been overturned, where composers have begun again at the very bottom of the spiral with experimentation at the level of sound quality and sound

134

production. There is no certainty, as he says. Minimalism rules. Consequently, he is neither willing nor able to prescribe the kind of music nor the manner of engagement that might be appropriate for his students. He can only ask questions; encourage experimentation; provoke debate. Inevitable as this appears to him, to Mrs Curwen it would doubtless seem a shocking waste of time.

I would suggest that this tension between instruction and encounter is both inevitable and fertile. These apparently contradictory aspects of human learning are the positive and negative poles between which the electricity of educational transactions flow. Encounter and instruction correspond with the left and right of the musical spiral, with the natural ebb and flow of musical experience. To some extent, it is possible to proceed by instruction in the acquisition of manipulative skills, vernacular conventions, idiomatic traditions, systematic procedures. Here, learning can be more easily structured and sequenced. But it is encounter that characterizes the left-hand side: sensory impression, personal expression; structural speculation and symbolic veneration. Here, the student needs to be left alone with possibilities, many of which will exist thanks to some instructional framing. Theories and practice of music education that fail to acknowledge a dynamic relationship between left and right leave us trying to clap with one hand.

Arts educators are easily driven into attempts to justify and explain what they are doing in terms of encounter, 'tacit' knowing. Malcolm Ross tells us that when we are experiencing art objects and events we are 'day-dreaming'. In music 'we sound the subjective world'. The teacher has to be careful not to wake the pupil and the 'teacher's clumsiness, insensitivity, nervousness and insecurity, all threaten the dreamer' (Ross, 1984: 52). But the arts are *not* a form of dreaming by any careful analysis of what dreaming is, as I tried to show in Chapter 3. To put it another way: they are as much dreaming as science is; they are part of the objective world of formulated ideas and presentations. Their unique qualities reside in their strong sensory impressiveness, their vibrant expressive resonance and their cohesive structural wholeness. In this they are the most powerful of the communicating media and therefore of vital communal importance. They are not private dream-worlds, though ultimately each of us makes of them what we will.

Recognizing the social element Ross sees the arts in schools as in need of radical transformation.

The classes would be jam sessions and the public events

community happenings. Arts lessons would generate an aesthetic dimension in the school's life — not merely function as yet another variation on an academic or vocational theme. There would be room for cartoon, comic strip, food, film, make-up, D.I.Y., clothing, the fairground, muzak, Boots Art, pop, electronic games, cars, bikes, hair, graffiti, advertising, entertainment, politics. The esoteric practices of the studio, the theatre, the concert hall, the gallery would be replaced by an altogether more robust, more plebeian, more ephemeral range of activities — all imbued with what I have called the vernacular spirit.

(Ross, 1984: 46)

There is something very appealing in seeing aesthetic experience as celebratory, illuminating every corner of life, vitally pulsing through the curriculum and corridors of schools. If we have any life in us at all, we seek out eventfulness rather than low-pressured sequences of dull routine.

Provided that people can opt in and out of such activities, schools and colleges can certainly contribute such events to the community. I can only repeat though: education in any compulsory form is essentially a process of active criticism, coming to grips with the various forms of human discourse through encounter and instruction. Schools and colleges only constitute a fraction of most people's life experience. It would be better to set limits to the tasks of institutions and the time which we spend in them. Ultimate encounters in the arts can be experienced by us more easily outside of classes, in other groups, by choice, perhaps alone, without conversation, tacitly.

Two descriptions of encounter

Case One: There is in Proust's great novel a description of musical encounter of great insight and sensitivity (Proust, 1913: 287–93). Unintentionally, Swann comes across a piece of music played on violin and piano.

At first he had appreciated only the material quality of the sounds which those instruments had secreted.

But then he became aware of the piano part:

Like the deep blue tumult of the sea, silvered and charmed
into a minor key by the moonlight.

The phrase itself, he tells us,

has the fragrance of certain roses, wafted upon the moist air
of evening.

Swann then begins to picture to himself the symmetrical arrangement and the strength of expression of the movement:

And then, suddenly, having reached a certain point from
which he was prepared to follow it, after pausing for a moment, abruptly it changed its direction . . .

After some considerable time, he comes across the piece again:

— and recognized, secret, whispering, articulate, the airy and
fragrant phrase that he had loved. And it was so peculiarly
itself.

Eventually he finds out the name of the piece and composer:

— as he held it safe, could have it again to himself, at home,
as often as he would, could study its language and acquire
its secret.

This process, this encounter, follows the developmental spiral: first
the sensory impression; then perception of expressive quality; then
structural expectations; then finding and declaring the experience
of this music to be part of his value world.

Case Two: In John Steinbeck's novel, *The Grapes of Wrath*, there
is a fine description of a musical encounter among people driven
from their lands by dustbowl conditions, living rootlessly in camps
by the roadside.

And perhaps a man brought out his guitar to the front of his
tent. And he sat on a box to play, and everyone in the camp
moved in slowly toward him, drawn in toward him. Many
men can chord a guitar, but perhaps this man was a picker.
There you have something — the deep chords beating,
beating, while the melody runs on the strings like little

footsteps. Heavy hard fingers marching on the frets. The man played and the people moved slowly in on him until the circle was closed and tight, and then he sang *Ten-Cent Cotton* and *Forty-Cent Meat*. And the circle sang softly with him. And he sang *Why Do You Cut Your Hair Girls?* And the circle sang.

. . . And now the group was welded to one thing, one unit, so that in the dark the eyes of the people were inward, and their minds played in other times . . .

And each wished he could play a guitar, because it is a gracious thing.

(Steinbeck, 1939: 83)

Here again the experiential sweep, from the excitement of bringing out the guitar and the sensory impact of the beating chords and running melody, to the vernacular and idiomatic songs and the expression of value.

The question is: can we devise a curriculum that guarantees such encounters? The answer is plainly, no. What we can try to do within school and college curricula is to bring about a state of readiness, so that encounters become more likely and more significant. Swann is prepared to buy a copy and work on the music at home to acquire its secret. Somewhere along the way there has been some systematic instruction and this is not the first time he has responded to music. Steinbeck's people are also prepared for musical encounter. They have heard guitar-picking before and they know the songs well enough to join in. There may not have been much instruction but there has been participation and the handing on of communal traditions.

The major task of the school and college is to increase the likelihood of these encounters by framing knowledge and experience in a systematic way in an explicit spirit of musical criticism, relating the music-making of students to the world of music outside, interculturally. Institutions can also make openings for encounter, by raising up celebratory events within schools, colleges, and local communities.

9

Generating a curriculum and assessing students

In summary

. . . no credible theory of music education can be sustained without an insightful analysis of music as an essential strand in the fibre of human experience. No sensitive practice of music education can take place without at least an intuitive grasp of the qualitative nature of musical response. No effective policy-making on curriculum content and evaluation or student assessment can be managed without a conscious awareness of what is central to musical experience. This applies as much to the curriculum in further and higher education as to schools. (Introduction)

. . . we need to plan a little more for consistency of effectiveness; we ought to have sensitively formulated curricula with a clear rationale. (Chapter 1)

We must avoid a reductionist attitude, imagining that we build up musical experience from rudimentary atoms: that, for example, we first perceive intervals or single tones and that musical lines or textures are assembled in our minds only after analysis of the component parts has taken place. The converse is surely true. Analytic description is a different perceptual and conceptual mode which may have some value, but may also divert us from phrase, from expressive gesture, from the play of musical structure, from the coherence and sweep of musical passages. (Chapter 2)

The arts are, and have always been, essential for developing and sustaining mind, as are other forms of representation, including language. And this development of mind is *intrinsically* rewarding, absorbing, exciting. (Chapter 3)

Art intensifies, draws together, gives us not the confusion of mere experience, but what Dewey calls 'an experience' (Dewey, 1934). When it is over, of *course* we feel a dislocation, a jolt, a coming-to in another world, not because the world of art is less real but because it is *more* real, more vividly experienced, more alive, more highly integrated and structured than most of our existence. (Chapter 3)

. . . we could accept the idea of a series of progressive development, even if we had doubts about the timing of this in respect of individual children . . . I want to suggest that there is a sequence, an orderly unfolding of *musical* behaviour, that there are cumulative stages through which the musical behaviour of children can be traced. (Chapter 4)

At least we might try consciously working with the grain of children's development, something that those rare and intuitively gifted teachers do almost by instinct. (Chapter 5)

. . . music can be culturally exclusive if the sound-spectrum is strange, if expressive character is strongly linked with a particular culture or sub-culture and if structural expectations are inappropriate. All of these elements, especially expressive characterization, can be amplified by labelling and cultural stereotyping. The task of education is to reduce the power of such stereotypes through a lively exploration of musical procedures, phenomena which can be relatively independent of cultural ownership. (Chapter 6)

What schools can never do is suspend the exercise of what Small calls conscious knowledge. They are unlikely places for dreaming, or for 're-establishing contact with the totality of mental life' (Small, 1977: 226–7). The strength of schooling lies, as Margaret Mead, Blacking, Popper and Bruner remind us, in the possibility of the creation of new values, in transcending culture, in critical reflection, going beyond 'first ways of looking and thinking'. (Chapter 7)

. . . education in any compulsory form is essentially a process of active criticism, coming to grips with the various forms of human discourse through encounter and instruction. Schools and colleges only constitute a fraction of most people's life experience. It would be better to set limits to the tasks of institutions and the time which we spend in them. Ultimate encounters in the arts can be experienced by us more easily outside of classes, in other groups, by choice, perhaps alone, without conversation, tacitly. (Chapter 8)

Rather than trying to muster a summary of the emergent thesis in a new form of words, I offer these self-quotations as a way of bringing together the main themes of this book. I hope it is now clear that I see schools and colleges having a special, though limited responsibility. They are or should be culturally subversive agents, investigating the properties of music (in our case), developing critical awareness, though explicitly framing knowledge in fairly systematic ways. Musical encounter is always the ultimate and general aim of music educators: but within classrooms it is essential to be able to recognize and respond to the specific details of musical experience, sensitively and positively. Music teaching can be effective only when the nature of music itself is understood and the development of students respected.

The issues for this chapter are the extent to which a curriculum can or should be cumulative, progressive; and the degree to which pupil assessment can be related to declared criteria.

Pupils evaluate the music curriculum

Figure 8 is taken from a study by Leslie Francis into attitudes towards religious education among 8- to 15-year-olds. In the eyes of some young people it appears that music as a school subject shares the booby prize with R.E., by comparison with other areas of the school curriculum. However, since this study is limited to only one comprehensive school and three of its feeder primary schools it would be unwise to make too many generalizations. Allowing for this though, Francis cites other studies of subject preference carried out during the mid-1970s to support his finding that, from the age of 10 onwards, 'music and religion consistently occupy the two lowest positions in the child's evaluation of the six curriculum areas under review' (Francis, 1987). These attitudes are expressed in response to the concepts 'friendly', 'pleasant', 'good', 'interesting', 'nice', 'happy', 'important' and their opposites.

Particularly striking in Francis' data is the slide in attitude from age 8, when music is second only to games in the high estimation of children, down to their views at around age 14, when it has the

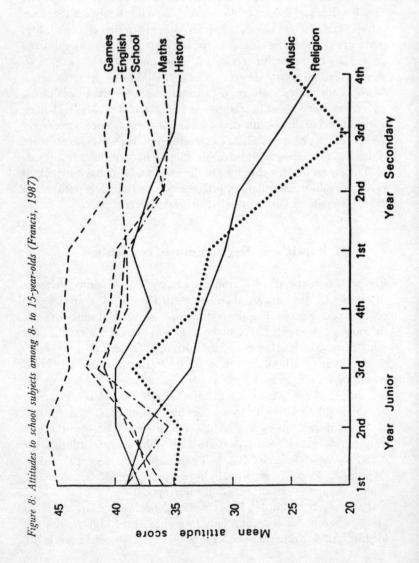

Figure 8: Attitudes to school subjects among 8- to 15-year-olds (Francis, 1987)

lowest esteem as a school subject. Why should this be so? In the case of music 'out there' in the community there is no doubt that young people over the age of 10 have a very positive attitude: it seems to be an essential part of life. It is school music that so often seems to have a negative profile among students, not music as such.

I am not here concerned with the frequency with which negative attitudes may be, found in our schools but with the reasons behind them when they *do* occur. It may be that music is seen not to be vocationally useful, as children move towards and through the secondary school. But what about games, which are surely just as 'useless' but are perceived so favourably?

Perhaps one major problem is that music in schools appears to diverge from music 'out there', both in idiomatic range and the social circumstances in which it is experienced. However we organize the experience and no matter how friendly, approachable or charismatic we may be; the institutional framing of knowledge is a constraint. The 'progressive' teacher is as much an agent of curriculum framing as the traditional 'director of music'. It is he or she who has decided to be 'child-centred', not the child. Music in classes is particularly difficult to organize to take account of individual aspirations compared, say, with literature or the visual arts: it is a social activity and must remain so to a large extent, even with the rapid spread of computerized keyboard stations within classrooms.

The divergent classification of music by style seems less of a problem in primary schools where teachers appear not to need to categorize music so readily into idioms, making less conscious use of stylistic labels University of London (Institute of Education, 1988). For those primary teachers who took part in our research, nursery rhymes, carols, hymns and action songs were the types of music most frequently mentioned, which amounts to categorization by social function and classroom use, rather than by cultural origin. This seems in accord with the developmental sequence. It is the broad vernacular, rather than the sharply idiomatic which characterizes children's earlier years, and primary school teachers seem to respond to this. Teachers in the secondary area were much more aware of idiomatic labels and were more exercised by the challenge of musical range. There are also sharper differences between pupil preferences and their own specialist musical education. The students too begin to notice: hence the frequently observed slide in attitudes towards school music. No secondary teacher can offer in a classroom anything but a limited selection of stylistic

possibilities and this clearly runs against the grain of pupils' development as they seek to enter the adult world, finding their own musical
niche. By contrast, in school games, the available activities can be
highly diverse, often taken up by choice, closely resembling what
happens in the real world; on playing fields and in sports centres,
what is seen on television, heard on the radio and read about in
the newspapers. In classroom music, what is feasible is a much
reduced realm of possibilities compared with the universe outside.
Choice is usually severely limited. Small wonder that young people
become disenchanted.

We found considerably more small group and individual activity
in secondary than in primary classrooms. In an attempt to respond
to the diversifying activities of older children, it seems as though
secondary teachers are trying to loosen classroom organization, to
weaken framing and, within the obvious limitations, to give more
choice, a recognition of growing individual differences. But consider the difficulty of range: instruments from various cultures;
specialist technical and stylistic help; spaces in which to work things
up; individualized listening facilities. Most of the secondary teachers
with whom we worked quite naturally felt themselves under-
resourced to meet such a commitment.

There is another element of difficulty. Several of the other curriculum areas, including maths, science and history, may also
appear to restrict individual choice and seem to lack direct cultural
relevance. But what they do much more convincingly is to communicate a strong sense of progression; they make demands. School
music lessons rarely seem to lead students on with any strong feeling
of purpose, excepting good instrumental teaching which has its own
built-in curriculum and sets of expectations. Class music seems to
be about 'enjoyment', a word frequently used by music teachers
and others who contributed to our curriculum study, though this
enjoyment must be limited by the circumstances of classrooms
which, as I argued earlier, are not the best places in which to
experience the peak experiences which music can induce and for
which ultimately it may come to be valued. Class lessons may or
may not be pleasant occasions but they cannot be relied upon to
reach those deeper levels of delight which mark out experiences in
the arts and it would be presumptious to assume that they can. Nor
should we forget the enjoyment of *achievement*: a sense of mastery;
travelling further from where we begin; the feeling of moving forward that can be experienced through good science or English
teaching.

It does seem significant that the students' own musical development appears to spiral upwards at the same time as attitudes to school music plummet down. We seem ill-adapted in our institutions to catch the natural surge of the currents and tide of musicality; perhaps because we have so far failed to chart them? Yet children are not inactive in our classrooms. Our research suggests that music in schools today tends to be a practical affair. Imparting information *about* music was an insignificant feature in the 32 schools we were able to observe. In comparison with other subjects, pupils too had noticed 'no paper and pencils', 'more movement than writing'. But does all this practical activity bring about learning? Is this learning cumulative? Does it feel like achievement? Is there progression? My impression is that this is fairly rare.

The problem of progression

One crucial difficulty for music education, along with the other arts, seems to be how to cope with the idea of cumulative learning; a concept now mandatory for the first time in Britain with the advent of a *National Curriculum* within which there have to be guidelines to ensure 'continuity and progression' (DES, 1987, hereafter to be called the 'Red Book'). In music, we seem still haunted by the feeling that the curriculum ought not to be too sequential; that a progressive curriculum might end up reducing musical experience to a series of exercises, losing the excitement of unpredictable encounters, that individual learning is indeed tacit. Brian Loane tells us that we must make no distinction between musical education and musical experience and that the teaching process cannot be gauged against a predetermined syllabus but by criteria 'thrown up by the pupils' music itself'. The music curriculum has to be provisional and revisable (Loane in Paynter, 1982: 205–6). In a similar vein, British music advisers warn us that 'real' musical experience cannot be acquired 'in a series of predetermined steps'; that such progressions do not take into account how individual children relate to music or allow for the development of a 'relationship between composing, listening and performing'. Furthermore, musical activity is 'concerned with the communication of feeling' and this cannot be predicted; we all relate to music in different ways (MANA, 1986: 15). So, following Bruner, MANA suggests that the curriculum will be a spiral, revisiting 'basic ideas and concepts with a progressively deeper insight', generating a series of encounters which 'leave room for the unpredictable, the original, and even the idiosyncratic'.

This may be so but we are left in some doubt as to what these ideas and 'concepts' might be. What is to make up the actual content of the curriculum spiral? And I remain a little puzzled as to what constitutes a deeper musical insight. Once again, teachers are left to decide for themselves and interpret broad 'philosophies' into daily action. Of course there is truth here. Each of us makes his or her own ark in which to voyage through life; among the arts music is especially personal and uniquely powerful; significant learning can never proceed by numbers; what is not felt as encounter is not felt at all. But there are musical criteria in the world that exist along with those 'thrown up' by pupils' own music-making: there are other musicians at work 'out there' making their contribution to what Popper calls 'World Three'. To some extent and before any of us is born there is already an agenda of musical practices, procedures and ideas which *in themselves* must contribute to the content and structure of the education. But these procedures and ideas are not 'concepts' in the usual meaning of that word (see Regelski, 1986).

Concepts or features?

Concepts are the product of a cognitive process 'which is characterized by the thinking of qualities, aspects, and relations of objects, at which therefore comparison, generalization, abstraction, and reasoning become possible' (Drever, 1952). Essentially, a concept is a property we hold in mind which allows us to cluster, classify and categorize experience, seeing certain things as similar or different in a particular way. Conceptualization is the beginning of theoretical description and organization. For example: many pieces of music share the property of being in a minor mode; other pieces may have in common triple metre or perhaps ternary structure. It is tempting to organize a curriculum around such concepts, as do the writers of the *Manhattanville Music Curriculum Program* (1970). By taking concept areas, organizing principles, such as rhythm, pitch, timbre and form, it becomes possible to see how a course of musical study could be fleshed out in an apparently progressive way, re-visiting each concept area at different levels of achievement.

But how do concepts relate to musical experience; to what Polanyi would call 'dwelling in' music? They are at best critical generalizations that we are able to form after a number of musical encounters: at worst they become substitutes for musical experience.

On analysis, 'concepts' usually turn out to be either parcels of information, knowing 'that', or aural skills of identification, knowing 'how'. If after listening to a recording of a blues sung by Bessie Smith, someone tells us that it was (more or less) in a minor key, would we say that he or she had a concept of 'minor'? We probably would. What is being demonstrated is some degree of aural discrimination along with a knowledge of appropriate technical terminology. These are not the essentials of musical experience, the knowing 'this' of encounter; nor are they by themselves sufficiently interesting bits of knowing to take us much further.

The trouble with such concepts is that they only pick up fragments of the total experience: we lost the sense of the whole in making explicit what was once tacitly apprehended. To take an analogy: I have a concept of 'noses', I know what physiological purpose they serve, that most if not all animals have them and that they come in a range of shapes and sizes. But the strong aquiline nose of a friend is a striking *feature*, not a concept. A feature is a distinctive and distinguishing element; a concept is a generalization. A concept draws attention to what is commonplace; a feature strikes us with what is unique in its context. Thus, the falling semitone that haunts the song about the dying rose in Britten's *Serenade for Tenor, Horn and Strings* is a feature of that movement. Repeating falling semitones is a common enough expressive device but this song is *not* an illustration of the technique but a new embodiment of it in a special context.

A danger with 'concepts' is that we tend to work from them and to them, looking for music which exemplifies their characteristics. This can diminish whatever prospect there may be for musical encounters in classrooms, as though music was merely an illustration of something else. So I might choose to rehearse a song because it demonstrated the concept of 'changing metre', whereas the only good reasons for choosing anything are that it has musical potential (I have taken some trouble to define what musical potential might be) and is within the vocal and emotional range of the students.

An alternative way of working has been described elsewhere (Swanwick and Taylor, 1982). The process is to start wherever possible with a likely musical encounter; through composition, performance or audience listening. Each activity might then follow the experiential sequence. A teacher might at some time have been impressed by the Britten song in his or her own musical explorations. Students too can work with falling semitones, investigating

147

something of their sensory possibilities when played in different registers or at different speeds and loudness and even when combined into dissonance; acquiring an element of manipulative mastery moving off into the domain of expressive potential that is inherent in the interval, noticing its effect in other pieces, in the vernacular around them; learning how to integrate the idea with new material in acts of musical speculation. If they are in secondary school, they should be able to use and perceive the device as a feature within different musical styles. At some point it may be that the students come to listen in audience to the music which fired the imagination of someone, in this case the teacher: if so, then they will certainly come to it with a background of experience that will have them more ready for potential encounter.

Of course, by the end of all this, 'falling semitones' might indeed have become a 'concept', a generalized abstraction, and may appear as such in a music curriculum document. But if falling semitones are regarded *only* in this way we are likely to forget their origins as expressive features encountered in 'real' music. Their impressiveness must not be lost in the interests of curriculum tidiness.

Over a period of time, we might build up several musical features into sequential order as a curriculum outline with a degree of progression. Thus, it seems likely that working with a pentatonic scale for the first time would usually precede composition with a more extensive note-row: that drones would be handled earlier than a blues or any other chord sequence; that metric rhythm patterns might be sequenced by complexity and length or that some intervals — perhaps parallel fifths or thirds — would be explored in advance of chords. New technology in the form of synthesizers and computers has great potential here in helping us to isolate and generate particular sound sets; abstracting edge tones, sound envelopes, levels of attack and decay, patterns of harmonic distribution, varieties of timbre, and so on; though we need to go beyond these.

Sets of sound will be the candidates for our 'concept' lists. From these beginnings the day-to-day activities of the music curriculum can spiral upward. Each sound-set starts off a small project; each beginning is new and fresh, though made possible by previous work. From these points of entry, the activities of composing, performing and audience-listening take us through the developmental or experiential sequence. The music curriculum is then at once modular and sequential, in that each set of sound, though in itself the germ of a module, is progressively related to those experienced before and after. And within each module there is also a sequence of development, of progression. Here is work for the future: building up the substance of this curriculum is a distinctive contribution that practising teachers can make. It may then be that the pupils' evaluation of music in the curriculum becomes more positive. There is a bonus that accrues from this way of working. When the curriculum is less arbitrary and some form of progression is admitted, pupil assessment becomes feasible, meaningful and fair.

Assessment in the arts

Arts educators sometimes appear less than clear about what they are up to. Are the arts important human activities or aren't they? Are they really only a kind of dreaming? Is there something to learn and therefore to teach or isn't there? If there is something to learn, can we see when it has been learned or is the learning invisible? Many arts teachers feel great sympathy with Michael Polanyi when he says 'we can know more than we can tell', but then many scientists might say the same.

As I tried to show earlier, the very idea of tacit knowledge appears to be totally opposed to the notion of pre-specified and observable learning and against measurable objectives. If we can't see learning, how can we assess it? Is this why even the 'Red Book' indicates that the arts need only to have curriculum 'guidelines' rather than 'clear objectives'? Are the arts once again to be marginalized?

At this point we stand once again at the crossroads, contemplating whether to follow the signs towards 'instruction' or 'encounter'. We can say, following Ross, that the arts are essentially subjective dream-worlds, within which we try to resolve our own 'sensate problems'. If such a route is followed, then assessment of any kind becomes anathema. I regard this attitude as not only politically unwise, but worse, theoretically unsound. Such a view invalidates the whole idea of education in the arts. How can we teach what we do not understand? How can we respond to students in any meaningful way without assessing what they do, make or say?

The alternative way is to acknowledge that to teach *is* to assess, to weigh up, to appraise; in order more adequately to plan for and facilitate richer response, to accept that arts teaching is arts criticism. The arts are not to be thought of as the last bastion against explanation, a mysterious area of ritual, a domain of magic, impossible to analyse without destroying the sacred mystery of 'wholeness' and 'vision'. Understanding how the arts affect us and the parameters within which we might assess artistic work is a quite different activity from directly responding to an art object or event. When we stand before a work our response is, or should be, an open encounter, intuitive, 'holistic' and our knowledge of its components will be primarily 'tacit', unanalysed. But if we are to begin to articulate ideas *about* this experience to others — perhaps a student, a colleague, a parent or an external assessor — then critical analysis is inevitable. There must be declared criteria which, though they may evolve over time and constantly undergo revision, should be steady enough to limit arbitrary judgements. Understanding something of how we develop our capacity to make and respond to art can only illuminate teaching, infuse quality into curriculum practice and play a part in making assessment valid and reliable.

We have to be sure though that appropriate and sensitive assessment practices are developed. 'Tests' which turn out to be no more than paper and pencil exercises will bear little relationship to the real world of artists, musicians, painters and designers, dancers, writers, actors and playwrights? What test would be realistic for assessing E.M. Forster's ability as a novelist; Rembrandt as a painter; Ravi Shankir as a musician or even Rutherford as a scientist? Testing in the simplistic sense will never be of much if any value to us. We ought, though, to be able to sustain an alternative vision of assessment as an extension of teaching, assessment as *criticism*; appraisal of the folio, the poem, the dance, the improvisation, the performance, the composition, the design, the artifact; all those objects and events in the real world.

Developing musical criteria

If we are to seek to assess students' work from the stance of sensitive critics, then we need to become more explicit about our criteria. Without criteria, communication with students is likely to be rudimentary and we shall certainly fail to articulate our judgements clearly to the outside world, from when come demands for accountability. From where are these criteria to be drawn? The answer seems often to be: 'out of the air'. It has been interesting to see the recent belated burgeoning of criteria in Britain, especially in relation to the demands of the GCSE examination, as groups of educators have come together to draft papers, often lacking serviceable theoretical models and influenced somewhat fitfully by work in the field. For instance, though the concepts of expression and structure have been drawn into the GCSE National Criteria and taken up by the music examining boards, their musical import and the implications for assessment seem to be little developed.

The London and East Anglian Group, for example, have produced a list of criteria for composition (LEAG, 1987): maintaining a style, exploitation of the medium, impact and overall impression, are considered obligatory. But the last of these lies in quite a different conceptual category from the others. 'Impact and overall impression' is not a criterion as the others are; the phrase lacks the objectivity which is the essence of a criterion statement and, in any case surely includes the other criteria? A further list, including melody, notation, medium, tempo and texture, is laid down with instructions for examiners to give marks under no fewer than three and no more than five headings. These separate marks are then to be totalled to a grade. Adding up marks awarded under a checklist system seems an odd way to engage in musical criticism.

A booklet, *Underway with GCSE Music* (LEAG, 1987), gives further advice to help teachers adapt their curriculum to the new examination scheme. Here again we meet criteria; this time for improvisation. These are overall form, melodic, harmonic or rhythmic development and adherence to the set style (p. 38). A little reflection on these will show up deficiencies. Can 'form' really be split up into 'overall' and 'development'; does not the overall form come out of the detailed relationships, for instance, the similarity or contrast of phrases? Does it matter that expressive character is not taken up at all into the accounting system for improvisation?

I am not generally encouraged by the examples of 'grade descriptions' to be found among the various boards. To be useful, criteria statements should indicate qualitative differences rather than quantitative shifts. It is not so difficult to devise these descriptions, provided that there is a shared and serviceable model of musical criticism, *an adequate theory*. I would offer the following way of generating criterion statements as a starting point for discussion, related, of course, to the theory of musical engagement developed in this book.

The secret is to take the right-hand side of the spiral, the 'public' or social side, and find descriptions for *manipulative, vernacular* and *idiomatic*. By definition, the manipulative mode is to do with basic control of sound materials, while the vernacular is about the exploitation of materials within the more demanding context of broad musical conventions: idiomatic musical achievement requires even greater control inside a consistent style. There are then three qualitatively different levels of musical control: *minimal materials* (manipulative) centres on the ability to repeat sounds, for instance to hold a steady pulse; *limited materials* (vernacular) describes the ability to produce conventional patterns, perhaps phrases; *technically developed materials* (idiomatic) indicates that recognizable stylistic devices have been assimilated into the repertory of musical action. From these points of critical judgement it is possible to begin to describe the related elements on the left-hand side of the spiral.

The levels of the grade suggested here are negotiable, as are the details of the descriptions; but the dynamic structure is drawn from closely studying children, analysis of psychological observations and numerous reflections on music and musical experience. An alternative structure would require an alternative theory.

Possible GCSE grade-related criteria for **composing/improvising**

Grade G: SENSORY   Intermittent control of minimal musical materials is associated with little or no expressive characterization. There are no identifiable structural relationships and the evolution of the composition may depend heavily on technical accidents which are not exploited.

Grade F: MANIPULATIVE   Minimal materials are carefully negotiated with little expressive characterization. The musical ordering may be arbitrary, rambling or repetitious and will lack cohesion and internal logic.

Grade E: PERSONAL EXPRESSIVENESS   The mastery of limited materials, though not always total, is sufficient to make personal expression possible. There is clearly identifiable mood, atmosphere or gesture, though loosely organized in a fairly spontaneous manner.

Grade D: VERNACULAR   A limited range of materials is managed consistently. The vocabulary of expression lies within recognizable musical conventions. There may be much repetition but will be little contrast or development, and the course of the music will be fairly predictable.

Grade C: SPECULATIVE   Limited musical materials are generally well handled. Expressive characterization may be fairly conventional but will be structured in interesting, possibly experimental ways. There may be variation, transformation and contrast of musical ideas and the work has the potential to hold the attention.

Grade B: IDIOMATIC   Technically developed materials embody expressive and structural elements organized within a coherent musical style. There will be imaginative structural juxtapositions taking place over a time period long enough to demonstrate an ability to sustain and develop musical thought.

Grade A: SYMBOLIC   Technical mastery serves musical communication. The listener's attention is focused on formal relationships and expressive character which are fused together in an impressive, coherent and original musical statement, made with commitment.

Along these same lines, it would be relatively easy to draw up criteria for performance and it even becomes possible to attempt to construct criteria for 'listening', the most difficult area. The latter might look something like this.

Possible GCSE grade-related criteria for **listening**

Grade G: SENSORY   The student recognizes clear difference of loudness level; widely different pitch differences; obvious changes of tone colour and texture. None of these is technically analysed and there is no account of expressive character or structural relationships.

Grade F: MANIPULATIVE   The student identifies, but does not analyse, devices to do with the management of musical material: for example, trills; *tremolos*; scalic patterns; *glissandi*; steady or fluctuating beat; spatial and stereophonic effects; like and unlike instrumental sounds.

Grade E: PERSONAL EXPRESSIVENESS   The student describes the general atmosphere, mood or character of a passage and recognizes changes of expressive level, without drawing attention to structural relationships. Descriptions of the

153

music may be in terms of dramatic incident, stories, personal associations and visual images, or feeling qualities.

Grade D: VERNACULAR   The student recognizes common musical procedures and may identify such elements as metre, phrase shape and length, repetitions, syncopation, sequences, drones, *ostinati*. There is some technical analysis.

Grade C: SPECULATIVE   The student identifies what is unusual or unexpected within the context of a particular work and is able to draw attention to changes of character by reference to instrumental or vocal colour, pitch, speech, loudness, rhythm and phrase length; the magnitude and frequency of changes, the extent to which changes are gradual or sudden.

Grade B: IDIOMATIC   The student places music within a stylistic context and shows awareness of technical devices and the structural procedures that characterize a particular idiom; such as transformation by variation, decoration and contrasting middle sections, distinctive harmonies and rhythmic inflections, specific instrumental sound production or vocal *melisma*.

Grade A: SYMBOLIC   In addition to meeting the criteria for the other grades, the student displays evidence of personal exploration and commitment through an account of a chosen area of musical investigation. There will be evidence of individual insights and sustained engagement with particular works, performers or composers.

These 'for instances' of criteria are offered only to show that it is easier, more open and honest to derive assessment categories from a theory than to make them up as we go along.

Some may think that the whole business of assessment and criteria specification is an unnecessary intrusion into delicate educational transactions. At times this may be so; but we ought to remember that these devices are a form of *contract*, a statement of what is under negotiation in classrooms. It may be worthwhile to spare a little time and effort to draw up these contracts sensitively. In any case, we cannot now escape an obligation to declare our intentions and practices: whether we like it or not, the days of educational 'busking' are past.

Outside of the timetable

There is more to life than schools and colleges, and there is more to education than the curriculum. Institutions should resound with arts events, enjoyed for themselves, without syllabus structures, formal assessment or the trappings of criteria. The school timetable cannot contain the music curriculum, though maybe it should contain more than it does. The issue of 'directed time', of what a music teacher's contract involves, has to be squarely faced. Do we want schools and colleges to be communally alive or don't we? If so, then there must be opportunities for people to join in with and commit themselves to life-enhancing events and these must have space and time in which to evolve. Rehearsals for productions of various kinds and culmination in performance must be acknowledged as educative in the richest sense of that word. These events may not be in the National Curriculum but they are part of the National Heritage. As such they will not be assessed but *evaluated* for their richness as part of our cultural environment, the soil in which mind grows.

Sometimes, despite themselves, even official documents reveal glimpses of education that are visionary rather than cautionary. The following passage comes from the 1904 *Elementary Code*.

> The purpose of the Public Elementary School is to form and strengthen the character and to develop the intelligence of the children entrusted to it, and to make the best use of the school years available, in assisting both girls and boys, according to their different needs, to fit themselves, practically as well as intellectually, for the work of life.
>
> (Cited by Gordon and Lawton, 1978: 22)

For *the work of life*, not the life of work! This telling phrase captures an important emphasis. Such a resonance lingers in the air and has the power to permeate educational transactions even in today's world. For essentially, the work of life is the development of mind.

I have tried to show that music is psychologically woven into the fabric of human discourse; its presence in a culture is a postive sign. Our task is to fashion a genuinely progressive curriculum for everyone, at the same time as we promote unique events for some. This dual obligation, though difficult, is inescapable.

References

Abbs, P. (1982) *Education and the Expressive Disciplines. Tract 25*. University of Sussex: Gryphon Press.

Abbs, P. (1987) *Living Powers: The Arts in Education*, London: The Falmer Press.

Allport, G.W. and Vernon, P.E. (1935) *Studies in Expressive Movement*, New York: Macmillan.

Asch, S.E. (1951/1958) 'Effects of group pressure upon modification and distortion of judgements', in E.E. Maccoby, T.M. Newcome, and E.L. Hartley (eds) *Readings in Social Psychology* (3rd edn), New York: Holt, Rinehart & Winston.

Aspin, D.N. (1984) *Objectivity and Assessment in the Arts: The Problem of Aesthetic Education*, London: National Association for Education in the Arts.

Auden, W.H. (1976) *Collected Poems*, ed. E. Mendelson, London: Faber

Bentley, A. (1966) *Measure of Musical Abilities*, London: Harrap.

Bernstein, B. (1971) 'On the classification and framing of knowledge', in M. Young (ed.) *Knowledge and Control*, London: Macmillan.

Blacking, J. (1984) 'Versus Gradus Novos Ad Parnassum Musicum: Exemplum Africanum', in *Becoming Human Through Music*, The Western Symposium, August, 1984, Connecticut, USA.

Blacking, J. (1985) 'Music making in Venda', in *Mana Mag*, Oct. 1985.

Blacking, J. (1986) *Culture and the Arts*, National Association for Education in the Arts, Take-up Series, No. 4, London

Bloom, B. et al. (1964) *Taxonomy of Educational Objectives, Book 2: Affective Domain*, New York: David McKay.

Bruner, J.S. (1966) *Toward a Theory of Instruction*, Cambridge, Mass.: Harvard University Press.

Bruner, J.S. (1974) *Relevance of Education*, Harmondsworth: Penguin Books.

Bullough, E. (1906) 'The "perceptive problem" in the aesthetic appreciation of single colours', *British Journal of Psychology* II, 406–63.

Bullough, E. (1921) 'Recent work in experimental aesthetics', *British Journal of Psychology* XII, 78–9

Bunting, R. (1977) *The Common Language of Music, Music in the Secondary School Curriculum*, Working Paper 6, Schools Council, York University.

Chapman, A.J. and Williams, A. (1976) 'Prestige effects and aesthetic experiences: adolescents' reactions to music', *British Journal of Social and Clinical Psychology*, 61–72.

Copland, A. (1952) *Music and Imagination*, New York and Toronto: Mentor Books.

Cross, F. (1984) 'From Rhythm and Blues to Reggae', *British Journal of Music Education* 1 (3), 233–45.

Curwen, A.J. (1886) *The Teacher's Guide to Mrs Curwen's Pianoforte Method*, London: Curwen & Sons.

Davies, B. (1986) *Social Control and Education*, London: Methuen.

Davies, J.B. (1978) *The Psychology of Music*, London: Hutchinson.

Delis, D., Fleer, J. and Kerr, N.H. (1978) 'Memory for music', *Perception and Psychophysics* 23 (3), 215–18.

Department of Education and Science (1981) *Aesthetic development*, A report from the Assessment of Performance Unit, Exploratory Group on Aesthetic Development.

Department of Education and Science (1987) *The National Curriculum 5–16*, London: HMSO.

Deutsch, D. (1982) *The Psychology of Music*, New York: Academic Press.

Dewey, J. (1934) *Art as Experience*, New York: Capricorn Books, 1958.

Drever, J. (1952) *A Dictionary of Psychology*, London: Penguin Books.

Dunmore, I. (1983) 'Sitar Magic' in N. Varadirajan (ed.) *Nadopasana One*, London: Editions Poetry.

Eisner, E.W. (1985) *The Art of Educational Evaluation*, London and Philadelphia: The Falmer Press.

Erikson, E.H. (1963) *Childhood and Society* (2nd edn), New York: Norton.

Finnäs, L. (1987) 'Do people misjudge each others' musical taste?' *Psychology of Music* 15 (2), 152–66.

Fletcher, P. (1987) *Education and Music*, Oxford University Press.

Forster, E.M. (1967) 'A note on the way', in *Abinger Harvest*, Harmondsworth: Penguin. First published 1936 by Edward Arnold.

Francis, L.J. (1987) 'The decline in attitudes towards religious education among 8- to 15-year-olds', *Educational Studies* 13 (2).

Freud, S. (1908) *The Standard Edition of the Complete Psychological Works of Sigmund Freud*, vol. 9, London: Hogarth Press, 1959.

Freud, S. (1953) *The Interpretation of Dreams*, Volume V in *The Complete Psychological Works*, London: Hogarth Press. Cited in R. Wollheim, *Freud*, London: Fontana, 1971.

Gardner, H. (1973) *The Arts and Human Development*, New York: Wiley.

Gardner, H. (1984) *Frames of Mind*, London: Heinemann and Paladin Books, 1985.

Golding, W. (1959) *The Inheritors*, London: Faber, published in Penguin 1961.

Gordon, P. and Lawton, D. (1978) *Curriculum Change in the Nineteenth and Twentieth Centuries*, London: Hodder & Stoughton.

Grahame, K. (1885) *The Golden Age*, first published in 1973, London: Bodley Head.

Grieg, E. (1905) 'My first success', an autobiographical sketch published in *The Contemporary Review*, July 1905.

Gulbenkian Foundation (1982) *The Arts in Schools*, London: Gulbenkian.

Hamel, P.M. (1976) *Through Music to the Self*, translation by Peter Lemesurier, Tilsbury, Wiltshire: Compton Press, 1978.

Hanslick, E. (1854) *The Beautiful in Music*, translation published in New York: Liberal Arts Press, 1957.

Hargreaves, D.J. (1986) *The Developmental Psychology of Music*, Cambridge: Cambridge University Press.

Head, H. (1920) *Studies in Neurology*, Oxford: Oxford University Press.

Hunter, H. (1970) *An Investigation of Physiological and Psychological Changes Apparently Elicited by Musical Stimuli*, unpublished MSc thesis, University of Aston in Birmingham.

Huxley, A. (1928) *Point Counter Point*, London: Penguin Books.

Jaques-Dalcroze, E. (1921) *Rhythm, Music and Education*, translation, London: Riverside Press, 1967.

Kakar, S. (1978) *The Inner World: A Psycho-analytic Study of Childhood and Society in India*, Delhi: Oxford University Press.

Keetman, G. (1974) *Elementaria: First Acquaintance with Orff-Schulwerk*, London: Schott.

Keller, H. (1970) 'Towards a theory of music', *The Listener*, 11 June.

Kodály, Z. (1974) *The Selected Writings of Zoltan Kodály*, London: Schott.

Koestler, A. (1964) *The Act of Creation*, London: Pan Books.

Langer, S.K. (1942, 1957) *Philosophy in a New Key*, New York: Mentor Books and Cambridge, Mass.: Harvard University Press.

Langer, S. (1970) *Mind: An Essay on Human Feeling*, Baltimore, Md and London: Johns Hopkins University Press.

Laurence, D.H. (1981) *Shaw's Music*, London: Bodley Head.

LEAG (London and East Anglian Group for GCSE Examinations) (1987) *Underway with GCSE Music*.

Lee, V. (1932) *Music and its Lovers*, London: Unwin.

Levin, B. (1981) *Conducted Tour*, London: Hodder & Stoughton.

Loane, B. (1984a) 'On "listening" in music education', *British Journal of Music Education* 1 (1), 27–36.

Loane, B. (1984b) 'Thinking about children's compositions', *British Journal of Music Education* 1 (3), 205–31, Cambridge University Press.

Lundin, R.W. (1949) 'The development and validation of a set of ability tests', *Psychological Monographs* 63 (305), 1–20.

Lundin, R.W. (1953 and 1967) *An Objective Psychology of Music*, New York: Ronald Press.

Maccoby, E.E. (1984) 'Socialization and developmental change', *Child Development* 55, 317–28.

MacCurdy, J.T. (1925) *The Psychology of Emotion*, New York: Harcourt Brace.

Mager, R.F. (1975) *Preparing Instructional Objectives*, California: Fearon.

MANA (Music Advisers' National Association) (1986) *Assessment and Progression in Music Education*.

Manhattanville Music Curriculum Program (1970) Bardonia, New York: Media Materials Inc.

Martin, B. (1981) *A Sociology of Contemporary Cultural Change*, Oxford: Blackwell.

Mead, M. (1942) 'Our educational emphases in primitive perspective', *American Journal of Sociology* 48, 633–9, reprinted in N. Keddie (ed.) *Tinker, Tailor*, Harmondsworth: Penguin Books, 1973.

Melly, G. (1970) *Revolt into Style: The Pop Arts in Britain*, London: Penguin Books.

Merriam, A.P. (1967) *Ethnomusicology and the Flathead Indians*, Chicago: Aldine Publications.

Meyer, L.B. (1956) *Emotion and Meaning in Music*, Chicago: University of Chicago Press.

Moog, H. (1976) *The Musical Experience of the Pre-School Child*, translated by Claudia Clarke, London: Schott, first published in Germany, 1968.

Murdoch, G. and McCron, R. (1973) 'Scoobies, skins and contemporary pop', *New Society*, 29 March.

Murdoch, G. and Phelps, G. (1973) *Mass Media and the Secondary School*, Basingstoke: Macmillan for Schools Council.

Mursell, J.L. (1948) *Education for Musical Growth*, London: Ginn.

References

Myers, C.S. and Valentine, C.W. (1914) 'A study of the individual differences in attitudes towards tones', *British Journal of Psychology* VII, 68 ff.

Newman, J.H., Cardinal, (1915) *On the Scope and Nature of University Education*, reprinted in Everyman's Library, London: Dent, 1971.

Orff, C. (1964) *Orff-Schulwer; Past and Future*, London: Music in Education.

Osgood, C.E., Suci, G.J., and Tannenbaum, P.H. (1957) *The Measurement of Meaning*, University of Illinois.

Owen, W. (1920) 'The parable of the old man and the young', *The Collected Poems*, London: Chatto & Windus, 1967.

Palmer, T. (1976) *All You Need Is Love*, London: Futura Publications.

Paynter, J. (1982) *Music in the Secondary School Curriculum*, Cambridge: Cambridge University Press.

Paynter, J. and Aston, P. (1970) *Sound and Silence*, Cambridge: Cambridge University Press.

Peters, R.S. (1966) *Ethics and Education*, London: Allen & Unwin.

Pflederer, M. and Sechrest, L. (1968) 'Conservation-type responses of children to musical stimuli', *Council for Research in Music Education Bulletin* 13, 19–36.

Piaget, J. (1951) *Play, Dreams and Imitation in Childhood*, London: Routledge.

Polanyi, M. (1967) *The Tacit Dimension*, London: Routledge.

Polanyi, M. and Prosch, H. (1975) *Meaning*, Chicago: University of Chicago Press.

Popper, K. (1972) *Objective Knowledge*, Oxford: Clarendon Press, new edn 1979.

Proust, M. (1913) *Remembrance of Things Past*, translated by C.K. Scott Moncrieff, London: Chatto & Windus.

Read, H. (1956) *Education Through Art*, London: Faber.

Reese, S. (1980) 'Polanyi's tacit knowing and music education', *Aesthetic Education* 14, 1 January.

Regelski, T.A. (1986) 'Concept-learning and action-learning in music education', *British Journal of Music Education* 3 (2), 185–216.

Richards, I.A. (1960) *Principles of Literary Criticism*, London: Routledge.

Ross, M. (1975) *Arts and the Adolescent*, Schools Council Working Paper 54, London: Evans/Methuen.

Ross, M. (1978) *The Creative Arts*, London: Heinemann.

Ross, M. (1984) *The Aesthetic Impulse*, Oxford: Pergamon Press.

Salaman, W. (1983) *Living School Music*, Cambridge: Cambridge University Press.

Sargant, W. (1957) *Battle for the Mind*, London: Pan.

Sartre, J-P. (1950) *The Psychology of Imagination*, London: Rider, reprinted in H. Osborne (ed.) *Aesthetics*, Oxford: Oxford University Press, 1972.

Schafer, R.M. (1975) *The Rhinoceros in the Classroom*, London: Universal.

Schoen, M. (1927) *The Effects of Music*, London: Kegan Paul and New York: Harcourt Brace.

Schools Council (1968) *Enquiry One: The Young School Leavers*, London: HMSO.

Seashore, C.E. (1919, 1939) *Measures of Musical Talents*, New York: The Psychological Corporation.

Seashore, C.E. (1938) *The Psychology of Music*, New York: McGraw Hill.

Shuter-Dyson, R. and Gabriel, C. (1968, 2nd edn 1981) *The Psychology of Musical Ability*, London: Methuen.

Sloboda, J.A. (1985) *The Musical Mind: The Cognitive Psychology of Music*, Oxford: Oxford University Press.

Sloboda, J.A. (1986) 'Cognition and real music: the psychology of music comes of age', *Psych. Belg.* XXVI (2), 199–219.

Small, C. (1977) *Music — Society — Education*, London: John Calder.

Spencer, H. (1911) *Education*, London: Williams & Norgate.

Steinbeck, J. (1939) *The Grapes of Wrath*, London: Penguin Books.

Stenhouse, L. (1975 and 1978) *An Introduction to Curriculum Research and Development*, London: Heinemann.

Swanwick, K. (1968) *Popular Music and the Teacher*, London: Pergamon Press.

Swanwick, K. (1971) 'Music and the education of the emotions', unpublished PhD thesis, University of Leicester.

Swanwick, K. (1973) 'Musical cognition and aesthetic response', *Bulletin of the British Psychological Society* 26, 285–9.

Swanwick, K. (1977) 'Belief and action in music education', in M. Burnett (ed.) *Music Education Review*, London: Chappell.

Swanwick, K. (1979) *A Basis for Music Education*, Windsor: NFER Nelson.

Swanwick, K. (1983) *The Arts in Education: Dreaming or Wide Awake?* Special Professorial Lecture, London University Institute of Education.

Swanwick, K. and Taylor, D. (1982) *Discovering Music*, London: Batsford.

Swanwick, K. and Tillman, J. (1986) 'The sequence of musical development', *British Journal of Music Education* 3 (3), 305–39, Cambridge University Press.

University of London Institute of Education (1988) *Music in Schools: A Study of Context and Curriculum Practice*, Project Director, Keith Swanwick

Valentine, C.W. (1962) *The Experimental Psychology of Beauty*, London: Methuen.

Vernon, P.E. (1933) 'The apprehension and cognition of music', *Proceedings of the Musical Association*, Session LIX.

Vulliamy, G. and Lee, E. (1976) *Pop Music in School*, Cambridge: Cambridge University Press.

Vulliamy, G. and Lee, E. (1982) *Pop, Rock and Ethnic Music in School*, Cambridge: Cambridge University Press.

Vulliamy, G. and Shepherd, J. (1984) 'Sociology and music education: a response to Swanwick', *British Journal of Sociology of Education* 5, 49–56.

Vygotsky, L.S. (1976) 'Play and its role in the mental development of the child', in J.S. Bruner, A. Jolly, K. Sylva (eds) *Play*, Harmondsworth: Penguin Books, 1976.

Wellesz, E. (ed.) (1957) *Ancient and Oriental Music*, Oxford: Oxford University Press.

Wing, H.D. (1948, revised 1962) *Standardized Tests of Musical Intelligence*, Windsor: NFER.

Witkin, R. (1974) *The Intelligence of Feeling*, London: Heinemann.

Wolff, C. (1945) *A Psychology of Gesture*, London: Methuen.

Wollheim, R. (1971) *Freud*, London: Fontana.

Index

Mager, R. 120, 124
Magic Mountain 45
manipulation 64
manipulative 67, 151, 152, 153
manipulative control 86, 116
manipulative mode 77
Manus Island 121
Maria Callas 97
Martin, B. 88
mass media 15
master-drummers 103
mastery 41, 43, 45, 46, 50, 55,
    57, 58, 59, 60, 64, 74, 89,
    144
materials 34, 43, 44, 47
    limited 152
    minimal 152
    technically developed 152
mathematical ability 49
mathematical thinking 106
mathematics 126
Mead, Margaret 105, 117, 121
Melanese pidgin 108
Melly, George 103
Menuhin, Yehudi 97
Merriam A.P. 114
metaphor 29, 40, 47, 66, 81, 88
meta-cognition 73, 74, 97
Metcalfe, Marion 8
Methodist 101
Meyer, L.B. 31, 63
Michael 116
microchip 99
military marches 109
mind 46, 49, 50, 82, 101, 104,
    155
minimalism 135
minimalist 57
modular curriculum 148
Moog, H. 54, 58, 59, 60, 66
Morris dancing 110
Moslem 101
Mozart 12, 57, 100
multi-cultural 3
Murdoch, Iris 47
Murdock, G. and MacCron, R.
    97
Mursell, J.L. 58, 59
music 94
    centres 12

colleges 12
    its cultural autonomy 107
    schools 12
music advisers 8
music and movement 59, 29, 84
music curriculum 90
music curriculum as a spiral
    145
music education
    aims of 118
music market 97
musical
    abilities 4, 54
    ability 33
    activity 13
    autonomy 111
    boundaries 98
    composition 60
    concepts 146, 147
    criteria 130
    criticism 5, 114, 115, 130,
        132, 151
    development 5, 54, 63, 81
    elements 22, 107
    encounter 81, 128, 141, 147
    encounters 127, 130
    engagement 13, 83, 151
    events 5
    expectancies 89
    experience 80, 89, 135, 145
    expression 66, 86
    expressiveness 72
    features 146, 147, 148
    gesture 65, 66, 86, 99
    ideas 146
    imagination 13
    instruction 124, 128
    instruments 106
    intuition 6, 18, 71
    knowing, 18
    labelling 91
    landscape 66
    language 134
    literacy 11
    materials 22, 67
    meaning 29, 74
    mind 4, 5
    norms 78, 89
    possibilities 118